Authentic Italian Cuisine

Authentic Italian Cuisine

A Practical Way to Cook Nutritious and Tasty Italian Dishes

Prabhjot Mundhir

Edited by

Kanika Gulzar Malhotra

Publisher
UNICORN BOOKS
F-2/16, Ansari Road, Daryaganj, New Delhi-110002
☎ 011-23275434, 23262683, 23250704 • *Fax:* 011-23257790
E-mail: info@unicornbooks.in • *Website:* www.unicornbooks.in

Branch : Mumbai
23-25, Zaoba Wadi, Thakurdwar, Mumbai-400002
☎ 022-22010941, 022-22053387
E-mail: rapidex@bom5.vsnl.net.in

ISBN 978-81-7806-385-0

Edition: 2016

Printed at : Param Offsetters, Okhla, New Delhi-110020

Contents

Acknowledgement *10*
Introduction *11*
Preface *13*
Foreword *14*
Foods of Italy *15*

Basics of Italian Cuisine

1. How to Make Egg Pasta by Hand 27
2. How to Make Basic Pizza Dough 28
3. How to Make Cheese Dip 29
4. How to Make Yogurt Dip 30
5. How to Make Bolognese Sauce 30
6. How to Make White Sauce / Cheese Sauce 31
7. Basic Pizza Sauce 31
8. Italian Bread Sticks 32
9. Pesto Sauce 33
10. How to Make Passata (Tomato Pulp) 33
11. Pickled Mushroom 34

Soups

1. Minestrone Soup 37
2. Clear Soup Served with Potato Gnocchi 38
3. Soup of Italian Marrow/ Cream of Courgette 38
4. Kidney Bean and Pasta Soup 39
5. Lentil Soup 40
6. Broccoli Soup with Garlic Toasts 41
7. Chickpeas Soup with Pasta 41
8. Mushroom Soup with Dry and Fresh Mushrooms 42
9. Roasted Tomatoes, Pepper and Fresh Basil Soup 43

10. Pumpkin Soup 43
11. Mutton and Vegetable Stew 44
12. Vegetable Stew 45
13. Spinach and Rice Soup 46
14. Italian Lentils and Pasta Soup 46
15. Asparagus Soup 47
16. Fish Soup 48
17. Minestronne with Rice 49
18. Chicken Soup with Vermicelli 49
19. Barley-Vegetable Soup 50
20. Chicken Stew 51

Salads / Insalata

1. Peppers and Pasta Salad 55
2. Sweet and Sour Onion Salad 56
3. Salad Italiana 56
4. Chickpeas Salad with Shallots and Black Olives 57
5. Whole-Wheat Pasta Salad 58
6. Roasted Potatoes Salad 59
7. Mushrooms, Spinach and Baked Beans Salad 60
8. Roasted Peppers and Tomato Salad 60
9. Tuna and Black Eyed Bean Salad 61
10. Roasted Chicken Salad 62
11. Crouton Salad 62

Antipasti / Starters

1. Tomatoes, Mozzarella and Basil Salad 69
2. Crostini 69
3. Potato Gnocchi 70
4. Gnocchi Alla Romana 71
5. Frittata with Spinach 71
6. Eggplant Fritters 72
7. Bread, Mozzarella and Tomato Skewers 73
8. Italian Cheese and Rice Balls 74
9. Cherry Tomatoes with Pesto 74

10. Potato Pizza 75
11. Eggplant-Walnut Dip 76
12. Roast Mushroom Caps 76
13. Chickpeas Patties with Yogurt Dip 77
14. Onion - Jalapeno Flavoured Cheddar Cheese 78
15. Risotto Cake 78
16. Baked Eggs with Tomatoes 79
17. Calzone 79
18. Bruschetta with Tomato 80
19. Fried Pizza Patties 81
20. Chicken Breasts Stuffed with Cheese and Ham 81
21. Prawns on Skewers 82
22. Chili -Tomato Cheese Toasts 82
23. Vegetables with Olive Oil Dip 83
24. Tomato Tart 84
25. Grilled Fish Kebabs 85
26. Batter Fried Prawns 85
27. Italian Meat Balls 86
28. Ham Sandwich 87
29. Melting Mozzarella Snack 88

Main Course

1. Multi-Coloured Macaroni in Cheese Sauce 95
2. Spaghetti in Meat Sauce 96
3. Pasta in Spinach Sauce 97
4. Three-in-one Pasta 98
5. Saffron Flavoured Chicken Rice 99
6. Ravioli 100
7. Lasagne Cooked with Meat-Sauce 101
8. Cannelloni Ripni 102
9. Polenta with Mushroom Sauce 103
10. Baked Polenta 104
11. Fish Monte Carlo 104
12. Italian Bread 105
13. Linguini with Mixed Peppers 107

14. Mutton Olives 107
15. Red Chili Pasta 109
16. Chicken with Basil Cream Sauce 110
17. Fish Fillets Grilled on Rotisserie 110
18. Bow Pasta with Green Pesto Sauce....................111
19. Chicken Italiana....................112
20. Fried Fish....................113
21. Stuffed Peppers....................114
22. Risotto with Vegetables and Roasted Chicken....................115
23. Lemon Fish....................115
24. Roasted Tomatoes and Garlic....................116
25. Focaccia....................117
26. Chicken Cooked with Red Grapes....................117
27. Prawns Cooked in Their Shells....................118
28. Turkey Rolls....................119
29. Pumpkin Chicken Pie....................120
30. Tomato Rice....................121
31. Roasted Chicken with Lemon and Vegetables....................122
32. Mushroom Stuffed Baked Chicken Rolls....................122
33. Chili-Garlic Flavoured Broccoli....................124
34. Garlc Flavoured Prawns Rissotto....................124
35. Grilled Zucchini with Pines....................125
36. Chicken-balls in Chili-Garlic Sauce....................125
37. Lasagne Cooked with Spinach Sauce....................126
38. Peppers Cooked in Rome Style....................127
39. Tagliated Mushroom Pasta with Mushroom Sauce....................128
40. Stuffed Tomatoes with Pasta....................128
41. Stuffed Cabbage Rolls....................129
42. Sweet-n-Sour Aubergines....................130
43. Chicken Roasted with Wine and Herbs....................131

Desserts

1. Lemon Soufflé....................137
2. Apple Cake....................138
3. Vanilla Custard Ice Cream....................139

4. Stuffed Peaches 140
5. Lemon- Cheese Cake 141
6. Baked Apples with Red Wine 141
7. Walnut-Orange-Ricotta Cake 142
8. Orange Granita 143
9. Tiramisu......144
10. Fruit salad......144
11. Cenci 145
12. Italian Cookies......146
13. Sesame Cookies......146
14. Coffee Granita......147
15. Choco Roll 148
16. Apple Tart......149
17. Lemon Ice Cream with Walnuts......150
18. Italian Trifle 150
19. Home-Made Hazelnut Ice Cream......151
20. Zabaglione 152
21. Chocolate Cake 152
22. Almond Cookies 153

Beans Peas

Acknowledgement

I dedicate this book to my grand children Amanat and Aaryaman and their generation that can't survive without creamy Pasta, cheesy Pizza and Chocolate cakes. Even during their cookery workshops, such items are high in demand. During tasting sessions these dishes are fondly enjoyed, and are polished within no time.

I also thank my students, family and friends who are source of my inspiration.

I always mentioned in my earlier books too, that I'm highly grateful to my dear husband Wg.Cdr. Mandhir Singh for his unrelenting support. Without his inspiration, co-operation and criticism, perhaps, I would not have achieved the excellence in my presentations.

Yogurt dip

Introduction

Good food has always been essential to the Italian way of life. **La Cucina Italiana** is one of the oldest cooking cultures in the world, dating back to the ancient Greeks and perhaps even earlier. The Romans adored food and often ate and drank to excess. It was they who really laid the foundation of Italian and European cuisine.

Italian cookery reflects the fact that the country was unified only in 1861. Until then each region produced its own characteristic cuisine, relying exclusively on ingredients that could be gathered, cultivated / reared or procured locally; as the Italians regard freshness of the ingredients more important than the diversity or innovation.

La Cucina Italiana remains distinctly regional, for example, northern Italian cooking incorporates ingredients that are simply never found in the recipes of Sicily and Napels. In the dairy farming north, butter is used in place of olive oil, whereas the most flavourable sun-ripened tomatoes, aubergines and peppers are still found in the south. The freshest seafood is found along the coast. The finest hams come from the areas where the pigs are raised and so on. The early Romans were peasant farmers who ate simple, rustic foods they could produce like grains, cheeses and olives etc. For them meat was unheard of luxury. Animals were bred to work in the fields and not to eat. Trading links with the other parts of the world encouraged Romans to cultivate new vegetables, fruits and vines. With their trade in salt and exotic spices enabled them to pickle and preserve all kinds of meat, fish and game. Food became an obsession and elaborate dishes were devised to be served in banquets for which Romans were famed. The decline and fall of Roman Empire led to a deterioration in the quality of cooking, a return to simple basic foods.

With Renaissance, however, came great wealth and a new interest in Elaborate food. Rich families started out do each other with lavish banquets where courses of rich extravagant foods were served and all were washed down with quantities of wine. Wealthier middle class developed a taste for fine foods and created their own bourgeois dishes. The finer features of Italian cooking even reached the French.

Italian cooks insist on high quality cooking ingredients like canned and preserved items, flavourful olive oils, traditional cheeses, pickles, preserves, canned and sun-dried tomatoes and bottle sauces. Now the variety and diversity of the Italian ingredients available in the super markets inspire to prepare any number of delicious dishes, from a simple dish of pasta to a 3/5 course meal can be arranged. In Italian restaurants a plate of antipasti (appetizer) followed by pasta or risotto flavoured with seasonal ingredients, then simply cooked meat or fish and finally a local cheese and fruit make a veritable feast.

In Italy pasta is an essential part of every full meal and does not constitute a meal on its own. Wines too, are important part of the sumptuous and tasty meals in Italy. The kind of wine that goes with the pasta depends upon what sauce it is cooked in. The general rule is that red wine goes well with meats and white one with poultry and seafood. Thus every area has its own special delights that make Italian cooking a real pleasure.

Prabhjot Mudhir

Basket of Fruit Vegetables

Preface

I was introduced to the Italian Cuisine in early 70s, when only a few selected restaurants in metro cities in India used to serve **Pizza and Pasta** along with some soups. The choice was never wide. Then the enthusiasts like me preferred to learn home-made Pizza base and sauce and started cooking it as antipasti for small gatherings. Slowly, **Macaroni and Spaghetti** were introduced in the market and magazines like **Femina** started writing elaborate recipes to cook them in satisfying way. Those were the days when ready-made sauces and other exotic ingredients were not marketed. Anyway that,s interesting history. By and by with opening of Catering colleges and chefs passing out from there, a great change took place on Indian scene. The principal of famous catering college of Bombay, **Ms. Thangam Phillip** was regularly writing recipes for **Femina** and that knowledge opened so many doors and brought flexibility in adopting new ways of cooking and making it integral part of life. Anyway, the defence officers were always open-minded and always appreciated new items on menu; and this is what encouraged the self learning; and it also helped to boost my self confidence. Well, well, 'the change is a law of nature' and the global change brought a revolution in total lifestyle; and the change in eating pattern is so imminent even in India.

Here, in this book the most popular recipes, traditional and contemporary, are selected which can be easily cooked by the enthusiasts and are commonly known to the Italian food lovers. Since Italians are warm, welcoming people who like to celebrate the traditions and festivals, so enjoy the gatherings either at home or in a restaurant with full gusto. They like simplicity and fantasy. Even the simple- healthy food prepared with basic tomatoes, garlic, olive oil, vegetables /meats, bread, whole grains, cheese and herbs is served with a lot of fantasy. Therefore, while developing the recipes and illustrating the dishes, the presentation also is kept in mind. All the recipes are tried and tested, I am sure you can't go wrong in attempting them for yourself and the loved ones. These days, thanks to the shopping mall culture, even the exotic ingredients used in any cookery are mostly available. With the global change myths have also given a way.

These days nutritionists say that it is a myth that **versatile pastas** are unhealthy. According to a global survey the Italian staple, pasta, has just been voted the **world's favourite food,** says The Times of India. Just as any other cereal, pastas can be added to salads and soups; can be prepared with cheese, vegetables and a variety of vegetarian and non-vegetarian gravies. A variety of meats can be added to enhance the taste as well as the food value and pasta can be turned into a healthy dish. The average person in Italy eats more than 51 pounds of pasta every year. An average North American consumes about 15 to 16 pounds of pasta per year. In the urban Indian metros also, the consumption of pasta has increased a lot in the past few years, as the working people of younger generation and the students living away from homes, virtually live on the variety of pasta in the form of take away food parcels.

Enjoy cooking and relishing Palatable and Sumptuous Italian Dishes.

Prabhjot Mundhir

Foreword

It gives me great pleasure to associate myself with this book of great clarity and conviction; I have known Mrs. Mundhir for more than a decade and have always admired her for her efforts in the food industry.

Italian cuisine is the mother of all cuisines and I am pretty sure we've had more Italian meals than French or other cuisines from the continent. There have been many Italian cook-books over the years covering almost all the recipes and cooking techniques, however this book scores in its honesty, deconstructing the myth of the difficulties of making pasta or risotto, as well as exploring the vast array of Italian cuisine with antipasti, soups , salads, main-courses, desserts and drinks.

This book is about cooking with love and pride and cooking for family and friends. The recipes are well researched and diverse, so the reader has a great variety to choose from, whilst being assured of the method and result of the recipe. Even those of us not born Italian can feel Italian when we cook from this book.

Italian cuisine is about using ingenuity to transform a few humble ingredients into sublime creations and Mrs Mundhir has shown just that. This book is a celebration of the cuisine and the culture of the great country of Italy we have come to love and admire so much.

Buon appetite !

Dev Malik

Grilled open cheese sandwich

Foods of Italy

Variety of Pasta in Italian Market

Lentils

Raw Chicken

Nuts (Used in Italian Cuisine)

Raw Mutton

Italian Herbs

Sun Dried Tomatoes

Fish Fillets

Peppers

Jumbo Prawns

Olives

Grated Cheese

Olive Oil

Foods of Italy

PASTA

Italy is home to some of the world's most popular and finest culinary products.

Of all the ingredients that describe Italian cuisine is ***pasta.*** Simple to cook but nutritious, in nature is the staple diet of Italians. It is made in different shapes and sizes and cooked in various ways with and without White / Cheese sauce, Vegetables, Meat sauces, Poultry and Seafood or simply tossed in Olive oil and lightly fried Garlic. It is used in Soups and Salads too. In short, in Italy pasta is an essential part of every full meal. There are two type of pastas, ***fresca* / fresh and *pastasciutta* / dried.**

Certain pastas, for example, for Long straight flat noodles, pasta for Cannelloni, Ravioli and Lasagne etc can be made fresh at home, but all the variety of dried pastas is machine made these days. Dried pasta is boiled first and then used.

Pastas can be divided into four categories:

Long strands——— variety of ***spaghettini*** /spaghetti

Ribbons—————— it is wider than the strands, eg, ***Tagliatelle and fettuccine.*** They are available plain and flavoured with spinach, tomato, porcini (mushrooms), chili and squid ink. The thinnest strand pasta is ***vermicelli.***

Flat——————————***lasagne and cannelloni*** are larger flat rectangle pasta. For cannelloni flat pasta is filled and rolled and for lasagne it is layered.

Filled——————————- ***ravioli*** is filled and square in shape; ***tortelli*** are usually round and ***tortellini*** are ring shaped.

Basically the difference lies in shape and size. While selecting the apt pasta for any sauce, though there are not any hard and fast rules, yet long and thin pasta is ideal for olive oil based and delicate seafood sauce. Whereas short pasta shapes with wide openings (conchiglie), spirals and curls etc absorb meaty and spicy sauces better. Almost all pastas are suitable for tomato based sauces.

GRAINS AND PULSES

Other equally important ingredients of Italian cuisine beside pasta are **rice, polenta and pulses** which are the part of first course of the meal. Mostly, short grain **rice/*riso*** is used because Italians believe that short grain rice variety makes the best risotto dishes. Rice is cooked with vegetables, meats and cheese etc. It is often used in soups too. Italians do not serve main dishes on the bed of rice but instead they serve plain boiled rice stirred with butter and cheese.

The grainy-yellow flour ***polenta*** (a kind of corn-meal obtained from ground maize), a type of porridge is used in various ways to cook the dishes for breakfast and main meals.

Pulses a variety of beans, ***fagioli*** **/ haricot beans,** are another staple of Italian cooking. Fresh and dried variety of beans such as **lentils/*lenticchie*,** kidney beans, black-eyed beans, broad beans and **chick-peas/*ceci*** etc are cooked like soups with or without small soup pasta or like salads with and without meats. Fresh and dry herbs are used along to enhance the flavour of the dishes.

Italians use a variety of soft and hard, mild and sharp **cheeses,** such as mozzarella (mild and soft) and mature flavoured parmesan etc in plenty. Italian cheeses are generally categorized in four sections: hard, semi soft, soft and fresh. ***Parmesan*** and ***Mozzarella*** are the most important of Italian cheeses. Other popular variety of cheeses used in Italian cooking are ***ricotta, gorgonzola, mascarpone, fontina and caprini*** etc. Almost all can be eaten on their own and used for cooking, too. Mostly:

Mozzarella— is used for stringy topping as it melts easily.

Parmesan— is mostly grated and used for pasta, polenta, rice and minestrone. It does not become stringy and rubbery. It is also delicious, sliced and served with ripe fruits and red wine.

Ricotta— is used in cooking for both savoury and sweet dishes. It is ideal to fill ravioli, cannelloni, gnocchi and lasagne.

Gorgonzola— is used for cooking creamy sauces for vegetables and pasta; for filling pancakes and for stirring in polenta.

Mascarpone—is used for savouries and sweets both. It is excellent for creamy sauce for pasta. It enhances the flavour of risottos. It combines well with walnuts. It is an essential ingredient of tiramisu, and is served with fresh berries or used as a filling for pastries.

Fontina—Because of its melting qualities, it is ideal for making cheese dip or fonduta. It can also be used in place of mozzarella. Of course, it can be eaten on its own.

Caprini—can be fried and served warm with salad leaves as an appetizer or crumbled over pizza as a topping.

Beside these names in cheese there are many more used in Italy in its cuisine.

VEGETABLES

Vegetables always are an integral part of any national or international cuisine, and Italian cuisine is no exception. They are served as dishes on their own in various ways; they are also used in salads, appetizers accompanied with dips, converted in soups and used along with pasta and rice. Asparagus/ ***asparagi,*** artichokes, cabbages/***cavolo,*** onions/***cipolle,*** fennel/***finocchio,*** aubergines/***melanzane,*** peppers/***pepperoni,*** tomatoes/***pomodori,*** spinach/***spinaci,*** zucchini/ ***courgettes,*** zucca/***squash,*** pumpkins, garlic, variety of fresh and dry mushrooms, wild and cultivated both such as porcini, chiodini, chanterelles, truffles etc, a variety of salad leaves, fresh beans, broccoli, cauliflower are the most prominent of all grown in Italy.

Note:

Of all the vegetables used in Italian cuisine, the most important is tomato. Use of tomatoes in the basic sauces is a must, either it is for pasta or pizza its use is inevitable. Like other bottled, preserved products tomatoes are available in all forms, eg. sun-dried, pureed, chunky and thick paste and that availability makes the Italian cooking easier to create healthy-delicious-sumptuous dishes almost instantly. Same way bottled mushrooms, peppers, beans, pickled vegetables, olives and certain variety of fish too, are easily available to dish out the hearty meals. Herbs available are mostly dried but are very effective in cooking.

FRUITS AND NUTS

After a full meal of different courses (***antipasto***/ appetizer, pasta and ***second do***/main course) Italians prefer seasonal fresh fruit to be served as a dessert on its own or converted into refreshing ***macedonia***/fruit-salad. Fresh fruits are also the base of ice creams/ gelatos, sorbets, granitas etc. Elaborate desserts are reserved for special occasions and often bought from ***pasticceria/*** pastry shop and ***gelateria/***ice cream parlour. Moreover, certain popular sweets are usually eaten with a cup of espresso coffee at other times of the day. Nuts and candid fruits are winter fruits, and are baked into tarts and pastries.

Amarena/ morello cherry, ***arancia***/orange, ***fico/***figs, ***limone***/lemon, ***melone***/melon, watermelon, ***pesche/***peaches, ***pesche noci***/nectarines, ***uva***/grapes etc are the main fruits grown and consumed in Italy.

Castagne/chestnuts, ***mandorle***/almonds, ***nocciole***/hazelnuts, ***noci***/walnuts, ***pinoli/***pine nuts and pistachio nuts are used in various ways in Italian cookery.

Hazelnuts are used dried in confectionery, cakes and pastries; walnuts and almond are eaten fresh and raw, too, when in season and of course are used dried as snack and in meat dishes, savouries, sweets, desserts such as cakes, pastries and ice creams. Pine nuts are used in many dishes, and are one of the most important ingredients of ***pesto* sauce.** Pistachio nuts are eaten raw roasted and salted as a snack, and are used in ice creams and cassata etc.

HERBS

The aromatic flavour of herbs and seasonings adds depth to plain Italian cooking based on fresh ingredients. ***Basilico***/basil, ***maggiorana***/sweet marjoram, ***origano***/oregano, ***prezzemolo/*** parsley, ***rosmarino*** /rosemary and ***salvia/***sage are important herbs; red and white ***aceto***/vinegar, ***aceto balsamico***/ balsamic vinegar, ***aglio***/garlic, green and black ***olive***/olives, ***capperi/***capers, ***peperoncini***/dried red chillies, dried red chilli flakes, ***zafferano***/saffron and ***olio di olive/*** olive oil along with necessary amount of salt and peppercorns are such ingredients without which Italian cuisine will not be considered complete at all.

MEAT AND POULTRY

A variety of **cured meats** such as sausages, salamis, bacon and ham are integral part of Italian meals. Every region of Italy has its own specialties of cured meats and sausages, each differing as widely as the regions themselves. Since ***Prosciutto crudo/*** salted and air dried ham requires no cooking, often it is served as ***antipasto***/appetizer on its own, and so are the variety of salami whose taste, texture and flavour reflect the character of the different regions of Italy.

Veal, pork, beef and lamb are the kind of meats usually consumed in Italian house-holds.

Agnello/lamb cutlets are mostly breaded and fried and leg is roasted.

Most Italian ***maiale/***pork is transformed into sausages salami and ham but fresh meat is cooked all over Italy with fresh herbs such as rosemary and sage etc.

Tender parts of ***Manzo/***beef are used as steaks and are roasted; and less tender cuts are either minced for making meat sauce/ ***ragu*** or meatballs/***polpettone,***

or braised and stewed.

Vitello/veal is the most popular meat in Italy. Young calves are slaughtered to obtain tender meat to cook as chops, cutlets or roast.

Along with the chicken, pheasant/***fagiano,*** turkey, quail/***quaglie,*** pigeon/***piccione,*** guinea fowl/***faraona,*** rabbit/***coniglio*** and hare/***lepre*** meat too are enjoyed by the large number of population of Italian countryside and urban area.

SEAFOOD, FISH AND SHELLFISH

Italian fish market has fish and shellfish of every description. They (Italians) like their seafood very fresh and cook it simply without elaborate sauces. Mostly, large fish are grilled or baked and then dressed with olive oil, and small ones are deep fried to crispness. Popular variety includes **monkfish, sole, salmon.** Fresh water fish eaten over there are **trout, perch, carp and eel.** Eels are considered a particular delicacy and are cooked in many different ways, from grilling to baking, and stewing to frying. **Tuna** and **sardines** are mostly canned in oil. **Swordfish** is either baked or grilled, **Sea bass** is the best when grilled, barbecued or pan-fried. **Red mullet** is Mediterranean fish and has almost prawn like flavour. It is regarded as a great delicacy.

Along with prawns, shrimps, clams, mussels, squid, cuttlefish and octopus are also relished in salads, soups and fried form.

DRINKS AND WINES

Italy is home to some of the oldest wine producing regions in the world. Italian wines are not only exported but also extremely popular n Italy itself. Italians rank fifth on the world wine consumption map. History tells us that Greek settlers produced wine in Italy before the Romans started their own vineyards in the 2nd century BC. Roman grape growing and wine making was more prolific and well organised. They were pioneers in large scale productions and storing techniques.

Aperitivi and Digestivi are very popular all over Italy. They are consumed at any hour of the day. The digestives are either aquavite such as ***grappa*** or liqueurs are flavoured with local ingredients. it is a pungent, colourless brandy and is not used much in cooking but it can be used for flambéing and for preserving fruits. The spirit takes on the flavour of the fruits; once the fruits are eaten, it can be served as a digestive.

Many of the vermouths and spirits are made from local ingredients, such as ***herbs, nuts, lemons and fruits.*** The Italians have great faith in the goodness of these drinks' digestive properties. There is ***limencello*** – a traditional lemon liqueur and ***amaretto,*** sweet liqueur, which is made from apricot kernels and flavoured with almonds and aromatic extracts. ***Fragolino, maraschino and nocino,*** respectively, are strawberry, cherry and nut liquors; and Nocino is made from unripe green walnuts steeped in spirit.

There are wines to pair with every meal. They enhance the enjoyment of drinking followed by sumptuous meals.

Amaro, a bitter aperitivo, is one of the most loved drink consumed before meals to stimulate the appetite.

All vermouths both red and white are made from white wine flavoured with aromatic herbal extracts and spices. ***Martini*** is one of the famous vermouths which is white and extra dry. Italians, mostly use white wine for cooking but martini can be substituted in sauces and in cooking veal, rabbit or poultry dishes.

Marsala, the rich brown wine is sweet in nature; it is matured at least for five years to give an intensity of flavour and colour. Dry Marsala is widely used by Italian cooks for flavouring veal and poultry dishes; and it is also used in preparation of certain desserts and patisserie. As a dessert wine, it is an essential ingredient of **zabaglione,** *alight froty dessert made from whisked egg yolks, sugar and marsala.* This wine made in Italy from grapes grown in Sicily has something in common with Sherry or Maderia, and contains about 24% of alcohol. It is drunk as an aperitif before meals. Its sweet version is served after a meal with little biscuits to be dipped into the wine it is also taken with a piece of choicest cake. It is very handy on the kitchen shelf as it has a long shelf life as it does not deteriorate once the bottle is opened.

A FEW WORDS ABOUT FAMOUS ITALIAN PASTA

Classic pasta is made only with wheat, semolina and water. To make Italian pasta, dried wheat flour preparation, mostly made from 'durum wheat' is used. The flour is well kneaded into stiff dough and forced through specially perforated cylinders from which it comes out in various shapes known by different names (macaroni, spaghetti, counchigliette, vermicelli, ditalini, ravioli, crescioni, tagliatelli and tortellini etc).

The variety of pasta is made by kneading vigorously hard wheat with boiling water. Then the paste is put in a bronze cylinder equipped with die and pressure is applied to it by a hydraulic press. The good quality pasta has a translucent, amber appearance. Egg pasta is made by adding dry or fresh eggs to the same dough mixture.

As we know that pasta, an excellent food, is essentially an energy food providing the body with 350 calories per 100gm pasta. The food value of pasta is the same as that of the cereals from which it is made. It contains carbohydrates and mineral salts, but only very small amounts of protein, fat and vitamins. To make pasta a well balanced diet food value is added by using milk, variety of cheese, butter / olive oil, vegetables and meats etc (which are seasoned with fresh or dry herbs) and all these ingredients provide enough protein, fats, vitamins and the dietary fibres to the meal.

Broadly pasta can be divided in four groups:

(a) Mostly small pasta made in the shape of alphabets, rings, stars, shells and rice grains etc is used in soups and salads.

(b) Straight-long pasta such as spaghetti, macaroni, penne, shells, spirals and butterfly shaped is boiled and tossed with a variety of sauces and gravies.

(c) Pasta for lasagna is boiled and then baked in layers with meats and sauces.

(d) The fourth category is pasta for filling; and in that category cannelloni and ravioli are the commonest forms. Cannelloni and ravioli are filled with a stuffing and folded; and finally baked with cheese sauce etc.

Cooking instructions:

Pasta, whatever its quality and variety, should always be cooked (boiled) in plenty of boiling water, so that it swells and releases starch.

To avoid stickiness after release of starch, add a spoonful of cooking oil and a little salt.

Small pasta is sprinkled in boiling water quickly, whereas long pasta is slowly lowered in boiling water without breaking the strands; loosened with a fork and cooked till softens.

The cooking time varies according to the quality and size of the pasta. Even if the cooking time is specified on the pack or in the recipe, yet it is better to test the done-ness of pasta before draining. Avoid overcooking. After draining, always rinse under the tap water and smear with a little olive/cooking oil. Keep it covered / warm in the serving dish before mixing with a chosen sauce.

The chosen sauce should be poured boiling hot onto the pasta. Stir with a fork, garnish with cheese or vegetables and serve hot.

Hard boiled pasta can be stored for a day or two under refrigeration but should be plunged into boiling water and drain again immediately before use.

NB: Since, it being their staple, Italians use a variety of PASTA to cook various gourmet dishes, in this book I have tried my level best to use maximum variety (available in India) of pasta in different dishes, so that the new learners/users are more aware about it.

COOKING METHODS OF ITALIAN CUISINE

In Italian cuisine a few vegetables are hardly used absolutely raw or directly as they are, or unless treated lightly in a certain way.

Peperoni/Sweet-peppers/Capsicums/Bell peppers: have a great affinity with Italian and Mediterranean food and each region of Italy has its own specialties using them. They are roasted directly on naked flame or placed under a hot grill until their skins are blackened and blistered, then placed in a plastic bag to sweat, so that peeling the skin becomes easier when cool enough to handle. Ultimately they are halved; cores are pulled; seeds and white membranes are removed to be sliced or chopped as per the requirement of the recipe.

Melanzane/ aubergines: are mostly sliced and salted for 30 minutes to remove the bitter juices. They believe that by salting them before use, aubergines soak less oil while frying; but they are used directly too.

Pomodori /Tomatoes: tomatoes are one of the vital ingredients of Italian cooking. One can't imagine any Italian dish without tomatoes in any region of Italy. A variety of tomatoes is cultivated, from the ordinary variety to cherry tomatoes, plum tomatoes, pumpkin shaped tomatoes to green tinged tomatoes for salads.

In case of tomatoes too, their skin is removed, they are deseeded and then used. For this they can be charred on flame, peeled, deseeded and used. Or to remove skin, tomatoes are pricked with a point of a knife, plunged into hot water for 30 seconds, refreshed in cold water and then the skin is peeled off. This way they are ready to be halved, deseeded and chopped or sliced for use.

Limone/Lemons: before squeezing the lemons, they are warmed gently, so that more juice can be squeezed. You may put the lemon / lemons in a bowl of warm water for 5 minutes, or place them in a microwave for 30 seconds on HIGH ie 100% power.

Courgettes: courgettes do not need peeling. They should be cut from top and tail and then sliced / diced.

Pumpkins and Squashes: they should be peeled and seeds and fibrous part removed.

Baby Carrot

Courgettes

Peppers

Mushrooms

Fresh Fruits

Onions

Basics of Italian Cuisine

Fontina Dip

Bolognese Sauce,

Yogurt Dip

Passata

Basic White Sauce

Pesto Sauce

Boiled Pasta

Tagliatelle

Pickled Mushroom

Basic Pizza Sauce

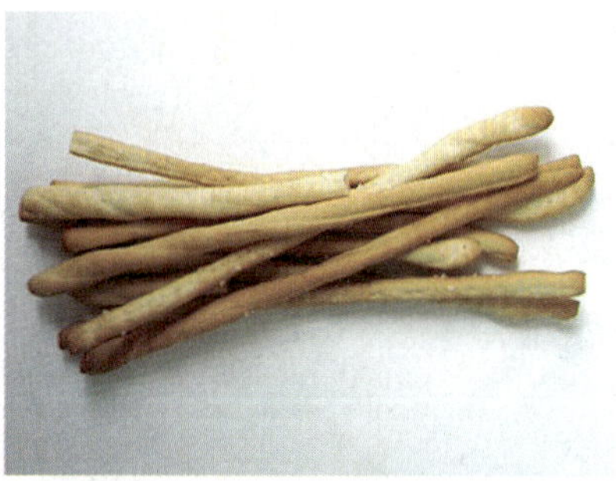

Grissini

Cheese and Fruit Display

Pizza Shells

Basics of Italian Cuisine

Note: Many dishes have been cooked in a microwave, but it is not necessary that you also cook in it. Microwave being an integral part of any modern kitchen, it has been used as a convenience. I like to use a microwave side by side just to save time. Please, you may use any electric gadget or a gas top for cooking heat. In that case Cooking time of dishes will vary.
Most of the recipes serve 4 to 6 persons, so it is not repeated again and again.

1. How to Make Egg Pasta by Hand

To serve to 4 persons

You Require:

Eggs	3 no	Cooking oil	2 tbsp (opt)
Flour	225 gm	Pinch of salt	
Or			
Flour	1 and ½ cups		

Preparation:

1. Break eggs in a bowl and beat them.
2. Sieve the flour and salt in a trove or on clean work surface; make a well in the centre and add beaten eggs.
3. Start mixing the egg and flour mixture with a fork or with your own finger tips. Gradually gather the flour as the mixture thickens. Keep mixing with your hands until it forms a mass. If it is lumpy and sticking to the hands, sprinkle a little flour and gather it scraping off the surface. Wash and dry your hands.
4. Sprinkle some flour on the work surface and knead the dough by pressing it with the heel of your hands away from you and then folding it over towards you. Repeat the action over and over again for 10 minutes or so, or until the dough is smooth and elastic.
5. Convert the dough into a disc; flour the surface and the rolling pin and start rolling the dough into a flat circle, rotating it constantly.
6. Roll out the dough until it is paper thin, stretching the sideways with the hands. Repeat the rolling and stretching process starting from a new point of the sheet each time, so that the pasta sheet remains evenly thin.
7. Wrap it on the rolling pin to lift it. If you are cutting it for noodles-tagliatelle, then un roll it on another flat surface on the kitchen towel, letting about a third of the sheet hanging over the edge. Rotate the sheet every 10 minutes and after 20 minutes or so pasta sheet will be dried enough to handle it for cutting the noodles.

8. To cut tagliatelle, fold the pasta sheet into a flat roll and cut across the noodles of desired width. After cutting open out the noodles and hang them on the back of chair for 5 minutes before cooking.
9. If you are cutting the pasta for lasagna or cannelloni, do not fold or dry the rolled dough. For lasagna cut it in rectangles approximately of 5-inch x 9-inch pieces; and for cannelloni you may cut the pasta sheet into strips, 3 to 4-inch x 6-inch in size.

   Note: These noodles can be stored in a cupboard for a

   few days after drying them completely, uncovered. Use them as required.

2. How to Make Basic Pizza Dough

Pizza dough is leavened with yeast. It rises once before being rolled and filled. The dough can be baked in Pizza pans or on a flat baking dish.

To serve 4 main course pizzas or 8 appetizers

You Require:

All purpose flour	3 and ½ cups	Active dried yeast	1 and ½ tbsp
Lukewarm water	1 cup	Salt	1 tsp
Pinch of sugar			

Preparation:

1. Take a big enough bowl that is warmed either in a microwave or by swirling hot water in it (drained). Place yeast in it and pour warm water; stir in the sugar and mix it with a fork. Cover and stand it for 10 minutes until the yeast dissolves and it starts to foam.
2. Sieve flour and salt together.
3. Mix half the flour in the bowl containing foaming yeast and mix it with a wooden spoon. Mix half of the flour (saving some to sprinkle on the working surface) and stir till it forms a mass and starts leaving the sides of the bowl. Remove it.
4. Flour the working surface; place the dough and start kneading it, working in the remaining flour a little at a time. Knead it for 10 minutes, by that time the dough will be smooth and elastic.
5. Form it in a ball; place it in a lightly oiled bowl; cover it with a clean-moistened kitchen napkin; cover the bowl and keep in a warm place for 1 hour or until the dough has doubled in volume. To test if the dough has risen enough, poke the two fingers into it. If the indentations remain, that means, the dough is ready to be used.
6. Punch the dough down with your fist to release the air. Knead for 1 to 2 minutes. Divide the dough into 2 parts to make 2 large pizzas or in 4 parts to make 4 individual pizzas.
7. If you are using a pizza pan, roll the dough about1/4 –inch larger than the size of the pan for the rim of the crust. Place it in the lightly oiled pan, folding the extra dough under to make a thicker rim around the edge.

8. If baking a pizza without a pan, press some of the dough from the centre of the circle towards the edge to make a thicker rim. Place it in a lightly oiled flat baking tray / baking sheet. It is ready now for filling and baking.

Tips:

a. These days, commercially, baked blind pizza shells are available made of flour or wheat which are just to be filled with choicest ingredients and baked,

b. The basic pizza dough can be used to prepare other recipes, such as, Focaccia, Breadsticks and Calzone etc.

c. The dough can be wrapped in cling wrap and frozen, and thawed before rolling and filling.

Variation: Whole Wheat Pizza dough

Whole-wheat flour	2 and 1/4 cup	All purpose flour	1 and 1/4 cups
Active dried yeast	1 and 1/2 tbsp	Lukewarm water	1 cup
Olive oil	2 tbsp	Salt	1 tsp
Pinch of sugar			

Preparation:

Follow the same procedure as for Basic flour Pizza dough.

Mix oil and half the wheat flour at step 3.Keep adding flour little at a time later. Proceed the same way till the dough has risen and ready to roll out and place in a pan.

Note: After applying the basic pizza sauce over the pizza shells, you may fill the Pizzas with only cheese/ cheeses, variety of vegetables, herbs, meats and seafood. Top them with mozzarella and bake in hot oven to the desired doneness.

Vegetables such as tomatoes, onion, peppers, mushrooms, courgettes, green peas and broccoli etc make good combinations with or without chicken and seafood etc. Of course you can always add on sliced jalapeno, black olives, baby-corn or corn kernels and sun-dried tomatoes etc (according to your choice).

3. How to Make Cheese Dip

(Fontina Dip)

This cheese sauce, cooked over slow fire or in double boiler over medium heat, makes an excellent dip to be eaten with bread.

You Require:

Medium fat cheese	250 gm	Milk	1 cup
OR			
Fontina cheese			
Butter	1 tbsp	Eggs	2 no
Freshly ground pepper	1 tsp	Chunky Bread to serve with	

Preparation and Cooking:

1. Cut cheese into small cubes and soak in milk for 2 hours.
2. Beat eggs lightly.
3. Transfer the cheese to a double boiler or to a heatproof bowl set over a pan of simmering water.
4. Add the butter and beaten eggs and cook gently, stirring all the time until the cheese has melted to a smooth sauce. It should have consistency like custard,
5. Remove from fire and season it with pepper. Transfer it to a serving bowl and serve it immediately.

Serving: Serve it with chunks of bread or soup sticks.

A good light salad and red wine accompany very well and make a hearty enjoyable meal in itself.

Tips: Fontina cheese melts better, so if available, use it for the dip. This dip is also known as Fontina Dip.

Cooking time: 20 to 30 minutes.

4. How to Make Yogurt Dip

Combine 2-cups fresh Yogurt (beaten) with 1-tbsp fresh chopped Mint, 1-chopped Spring-onion, ½-tsp White pepper and ¼-tsp red chilli powder, or ½ -tsp cayenne pepper together. You may add1-tbsp of roasted Sesame powder and a little Salt to taste. Chill the dip till required.

5.How to Make Bolognese Sauce

You Require:

Tomatoes	1000 gm	Olive oil / butter	4 tbsp
Garlic minced	1 tbsp	Mutton minced	300 gm
Mushroom chopped	6 no (opt)	Pepper	1 tsp
Chilli powder	1 tsp	Red pepper flakes	½ tsp
Italian herbs (Oregano)	1 tsp	Water or stock	2 cups or more
Salt	to taste	Meat balls	16 no (opt)

Note: Vegetarians can use Soy (soya) granules instead of mutton mince.

Preparation and Cooking:

1. Place tomatoes in a blender and puree.
2. Strain through a rice colander so that seeds are separated.
3. In a big micro-safe bowl heat butter for 1 minute on HIGH and add minced garlic; cook for 1 minute on HIGH and mix minced mutton; cook for 3 minutes on HIGH, stirring once in between. Take out the bowl and remove minced meat in a plate. Break the lumps if any.

4. In the same bowl combine tomato puree and all other ingredients for the sauce except oregano.
5. Cook uncovered on HIGH for 15 minutes, stirring thrice.
6. Add minced mutton and oregano to the tomato sauce and cook it covered for 5 minutes more on HIGH, stirring once in between. Let the sauce stand for 5 minutes before using it.
7. Sprinkle Italian herbs or oregano and chopped parsley or basil. Add meat balls and water.

   Info: This sauce is also known as Italiam meat sauce.

   Cooking time: 25 minutes.

6. How to Make White Sauce / Cheese Sauce

You Require:

Flour	2 tbsp	Butter	2 tbsp
Milk	2 and ½ cup		
Seasonings:			
Salt-n-pepper	to taste	Mustard powder	¼ tsp leveled

Preparation and Cooking:

1. Heat butter, add sieved flour and roast on medium fire to pale golden colour. Switch off the heat/fire.
2. Add lukewarm milk and whisk till the mixture turns smooth.
3. Cook on medium to low fire, almost 20 to 25 minutes, or till aroma of cooked flour starts spreading.
4. Remove from heat and season the sauce.

   For Cheese sauce: Add 1/4 to1/2 cup grated cheese and mix thoroughly.

   Do not cook again.

   Cooking time: About 25 minutes.

7. Basic Pizza Sauce

You Require:

Onion chopped fine	½ cup	Olive oil	2 to3 tbsp
Tomato-puree	1 cup or more	Chili-Garlic sauce	1 tbsp
Butter	1 tsp	Oregano	2 tsp
Pepper powder	2 tsp	Ajwain	1 tsp (opt)
Sugar	1 tsp	Finely chopped capsicum	¼ cup(opt)
Chili powder	1 tsp (opt)	Parsley chopped	2 tbsp
Bay leaf	1 no	Salt	to taste

Preparation and Cooking:

1. Heat oil in a pan and add ajwain (carom seeds) to crackle. Add chopped onion and sauté; add capsicum and cook for 1 minute on high fire.
2. Now add all the other ingredients for pizza sauce to it except parsley. Add ¼ cup water; mix well and cover with the lid. Cook for 3 to 5 minutes.
3. Take out the bay leaf; adjust the seasonings according to your taste and sprinkle chopped parsley. Your pizza sauce is ready to be used.

Tips:

a. If somehow tomato-puree is not available, you may use fresh tomatoes instead. Pass 700 gm ripe tomatoes through a blender, strain through a sieve and use. Only thing you have to cook the sauce a little longer till it achieves the consistency of sauce.

b. Instead of chili garlic sauce, use 1 tsp garlic paste and 1 tsp chili powder or according to the hotness of the chilies.

Cooking time: 20 minutes.

8. Italian Bread Sticks

(Grissini)

You Require:

Basic pizza dough	½ recipe
Sesame or poppy seeds to roll the sticks lightly	
A lightly greased baking tray	

Preparation and Cooking:

1. Divide the dough into16 to 18 pieces, roll with your hands and shape like sausages.
2. Place one piece of sausage looking dough on clean working platform and start rolling with fingers of both hands forward and backward to lengthen and thin the dough into a long uneven looking pencil about 1/4th-inch thick. Repeat the process with remaining pieces of dough. Try to roll out all pieces of same thickness.
3. Spread sesame / poppy seeds in a large plate scantily and roll all the pieces lightly. Transfer to a baking tray. Cover the tray with a cloth napkin and place it in a warm place to rise for 15 minutes.
4. Meantime preheat an oven to 200 degree Celsius. Bake the bread sticks for 8 to 10 minutes; remove the tray and turn the sticks and cook again for 5 to 6 minutes. Allow them to cool.
5. The bread sticks should be crisp when served.

Note: Crispness can be re-stored by warming them in a moderately hot oven for a few minutes before serving.

9. Pesto Sauce

For 4 to 6 servings of pasta

You Require:

Pine nuts	25 gm	Basil leaves	½ cup
Garlic peeled	2 fat cloves		
Coarse salt	a large pinch	Extra virgin olive oil	½ cup+1 tbsp
Parmesan grated	¼ cup		

Preparation:

1. In a dry grinder of an electric mixer combine pine nuts, basil leaves, coarse salt and garlic. Crush to a paste in on and off fashion.
2. Add grated cheese and just put motor in on mode and then immediately switch it off. Gradually add olive oil in it and run the motor slowly in the same fashion until the paste turns into a creamy sauce.

Storing: Store in a screw top glass jar under refrigeration. This can stay fresh for several weeks.

Tips: this sauce can be prepared in a mortar and pestle also.

Preparation time: 15 minutes.

10.How to Make Passata (Tomato Pulp)

You Require:

Ripe tomatoes	1000 gm

Preparation and Cooking:

1. Cut tomatoes into chunks and pass through an electric liquidizer. Put the motor on till the mixture is lump free. Pass it through a sieve.
2. Cook on high fire, stirring occasionally, until the mixture is reduced to one third or tomato mixture turns into thick pulp.
3. Transfer it to a clean glass jar. Heat 2 tbsp cooking oil to a smoking point; switch off the fire and pour over tomato pulp to seal it.
4. Screw the bottle and store under refrigeration.

Culinary use: Passata can be used as a basis for soup and sauces. It can be a substitute for fresh tomatoes in all the recipes where they require fresh tomato puree.

Cooking time: 30 minutes.

11.Pickled Mushroom

Choose unblemished mushrooms for pickling. Small ones can be kept whole and large ones can be halved or quartered.

You Require:

Mushrooms	500 gm	White vinegar	1 cup
Water	1 cup	Salt	1 tsp
Peppercorns crushed	½ tsp	Bay leaf	1 no
Coriander seeds	1 tsp	Garlic peeled	1 clove
Dried chillies	2 no	Olive oil as much required	

Cooking:

1. Place all the ingredients in a pan except olive oil and cook for 10 minutes. Bring the mixture to a boiling point and then simmer.
2. Drain the mushrooms but save the aromatic liquid and cool.
3. Put the mushrooms and liquid in a clean glass jar (according to the quantity) and fill up with olive oil. Seal the jar and leave for 1 month. Pickled mushrooms can last for 6 months and longer if stored under refrigeration.

Usages: Pickled mushrooms can be used in any dish to add flavour and meaty texture.

Tips: Don't discard the stalks; just remove the earthy ends; chop them with mushrooms or add to the soups or stock for soups and sauces.

Info: Pickled vegetables can be served with cold meats like Salami or Ham as an antipasto. Drained ones can be added to salads for a nice flavor. Their vinegary flavor goes well with cold roast meats etc.

❐

Vegetables with Walnut Dip

Soups

Mutton & Vegetable Stew

Chicken Soup

Broccoli Soup with Garlic Toast

Italian Lentil and Pasta Soup

Minestrone Soup

Chickpeas Soup with Pasta

Pumpkin Soup

Roasted Tomatoes & Basil Soup

Asparagus Soup

Lentil Soup

Minestrone with Rice

Chicken Stew

Clear Soup Served with Potato Gnocchi

Kidney Bean & Pasta Soup

Mushroom Soup with Dry & Fresh Mushrooms

Cream of Courgette

Vegetable Stew

Soups

Some of the best soups originated from Italy, as the Italians are great soup eaters. There, clear broth / soup, and delicate pureed soups are served as a first course before a main meal. More substantial chunky soups such as minestrone or kidney bean and pasta soups are often meals in themselves when the main meal of the day is at lunch time. The sumptuous soups are also cooked with rice and barley etc.

1.Minestrone Soup

(Minestrone alla Milanese)

It is one of the most popular thick Italian soups. The cooks there vary the recipe according to what is on hand, so one is at liberty to change the vegetables or meats accordingly.

You Require:

Vegetable stock	6 cups	Cabbage diced	½ cup
Carrot diced	1 no large	Potato diced	1 no
Onion grated	1 no	Garlic paste	½ tsp
Green peas shelled	½ cup	Tomatoes blanched	2 no large
Parsley chopped	1 sprig	Cheese grated	¼ cup
Cut macaroni boiled	1 cup	White pepper powder	2 tsp
Butter	1 tbsp	Salt	to taste

Preparation and Cooking:

1. Blanch tomatoes by cooking for 2 minutes on HIGH in a microwave. Peel and chop.
2. Heat butter on HIGH for 1 minute.
3. Put grated onion and garlic paste in it; mix and cook on HIGH for 1 minute.
4. Add all other chopped vegetables and stock; cover and cook on HIGH for 10 minutes.
5. Mix macaroni, salt and pepper; cover and cook for 8 minutes on micro LOW, i.e. 40% power.

Serving: Serve hot **'Minestrone Soup'** garnished with grated Cheese and Parsley along with thin toasted Bread slices. You may enjoy this soup with a burger or a hot dog, too.

Variation: Add boiled and shredded Chicken or chopped and sauted Bacon to the ready soup.

Tips: Minestrone is a thick Italian soup made of vegetables, chicken or meat and bits of pasta, and is garnished with cheese. You may use any small pasta for the soup.

Note: The recipe taken here is for the benefit of vegetarians, too.

Cooking time: 22 minutes micro cooking.

2. Clear Soup Served with Potato Gnocchi

You Require:

Well-flavoured stock	6½ cups	Egg shells	2 no
Egg white	1 no	Minced meat	100 gm
Carrot grated	1 no large	Salt-n-pepper	to taste
Potato Gnocchi	12 to 16 no		

Preparation and Cooking:

1. Boil stock in a deep micro-safe bowl for 12 minutes on micro HIGH.
2. Add minced meat and grated carrot.
3. Beat egg white stiff; crush eggshells; and put shells and egg in boiling stock.
4. Cook on micro LOW for 15 minutes or till all the sediments are gathered by meat, egg and shell mixture. Strain the soup through a muslin cloth twice and discard the meat-egg mixture.

Serving: Serve this water-like clear but tinted soup in a glass cup or a bowl as a starter with any meal.

Tips: Well flavoured, stock is made by boiling meat, bones & vegetables, bones and vegetables. Its water-like transparent appearance is full of minerals and vitamins. It is ideal to be served to young and old and sick and healthy people alike.

Though it is made of meat and vegetables, yet it is supposed to be very light in nature.

Note: The recipe of Gnocchi is given later in 'Gnocchi di Patate'

Cooking time: 5 minutes for preparation and 25 minutes for micro cooking.

3. Soup of Italian Marrow/ Cream of Courgette

(zuppa di zucchini)

You Require:

Courgettes	1000 gm	Olive oil	2 tbsp
Butter	1 tbsp	Onion chopped	1 no small
Oregano	1 tsp dry	Stock	3 tbsp
Dolecelatte cheese	100 gm	Single cream	300 ml
Fresh ground pepper	2 tsp	Salt	to taste
Fresh oregano for garnishing (if available)			

Preparation and Cooking:

1. Peel, wash and slice courgettes.

2. Grate cheese and keep aside.
3. Heat olive oil and butter together in a micro safe bowl for 1 minute on high in a microwave.
4. Saute chopped onion in it for 1 minute on HIGH.
5. Add sliced courgettes and oregano with salt and pepper.
6. Cover and cook for 10 minutes on HIGH.
7. Pour the stock over courgettes and cook for 10 minutes more on HIGH.
8. Add cheese (saving some for garnishing) and cook for 2 minutes on HIGH.
9. Liquidize the soup in a blender and pass through a sieve.
10. Add two-third cream and stir.
11. Check the seasoning and heat soup on REHEAT for 3 minutes.

Serving: Add remaining cream in the soup and swirl it with a spoon.

Garnish this creamy textured, rich soup with fresh Oregano and remaining cheese and serve it hot with crisp Bread.

Tips: Americans call courgettes-' Zucchini'.

Cooking time: 27 minutes micro cooking.

4. Kidney Bean and Pasta Soup

(Zuppa di borlotti-pasta)

One of the most popular soups eaten all over Italy, by young and old alike.

You Require:

Kidney beans boiled	2 cups	Small pasta boiled	2 cups
Tomato pureed	½ cup	Shallots cleaned	12 no
Tomato skinned and chopped	1 no	Garlic chopped	2 tbsp
Vegetarian stock	3 cups	Olive oil	2 tbsp
Parsley chopped	2 tbsp	Parmesan cheese grated	3 tbsp
Fresh ground pepper	2 tsp	Salt	to taste
Basil for garnishing			

Preparation and Cooking:

1. Heat oil in a micro safe large bowl for 1 minute on HIGH.
2. Add shallots and garlic, stir well and cook on HIGH for 2 minutes, uncovered.
3. Add parsley and kidney beans; mash beans with a wooden spoon; add tomato puree and stock; cover and cook for 15 minutes on HIGH. After 6 minutes, open the lid and add boiled pasta, salt and pepper. Cover again and cook for remaining time.
4. Stand for 2 minutes.
5. Open the lid and add grated cheese and basil.

Note: You may cook the soup on gas top / electric plate heat.

Serving: Serve **'Pasta and Bean soup'** hot with any Italian accompaniments.

Cooking time: 18 minutes micro cooking time.

5.Lentil Soup

(Minestra di lenticchie)

This delicious soup is considered one of the farm house / rustic soups of Italy.

You Require:

Dried brown or green lentils	1 cup	Olive oil	3 tbsp
Onion chopped fine	1 no	Celery sticks chopped fine	2 no
Carrots diced	1 large	Bay leaves	2 no
Rosemary dry	1 tsp	Basil dry	½ tsp
Tomatoes	4 no	Freshly ground pepper	to taste
Salt	to taste	Dry agilo	½ tsp
Veg / non-veg stock	5 to 6 cups	Basil leaves to garnish	

Preparation and Cooking:

1. Wash and soak lentils in plenty of water for 2 hours.
2. Drain the water and rinse.
3. Char the tomatoes directly on naked fire; remove the skin and chop them.
4. Heat oil in a heavy bottomed large pan; add onions and stir till transparent.
5. Add celery, carrot, bay leaves, rosemary and lentils; and stir fry for a while till well coated with oil.
6. Add tomatoes and stock. Bring the soup to the boiling point; lower the heat and cook for 1 hour or till the lentils are soft. To avoid spilling over don't cover the pan fully well. Keep it half covered.
7. Before serving remove the bay leaves. Season the soup with freshly ground pepper, salt and dry basil. Fry dry garlic in 1 tsp oil at medium heat and pour over the soup. Mix and keep it covered for a few minutes.

   Serving: Serve the 'Lentil soup' hot with garlic or any other bread.

   Variation: You may cut and fry a few Bacon rashers before frying onion and add to the soup.

   Cooking time: 1 hour and 10 minutes.

6.Broccoli Soup with Garlic Toasts

(Zuppa di broccoletti)

This soup is fondly consumed round Rome with garlic toasts.

You Require:

Broccoli	1 head large	Chicken/vegetable stock (well-flavoured)	8 cups
Lemon juice	2 tbsp	Salt and pepper	to taste
Bread slices	6 no	Butter	2 tbsp
Garlic paste	1 sp	Parmesan cheese grated	6 tbsp

Preparation and Cooking:

1. Wash broccoli thoroughly and break into florets; chop them roughly and place in a deep pan.
2. Boil the stock and pour it over the broccoli; cook for 25 to 30 minutes on medium fire or till soft. Cool slightly and pass through a liquidizer.
3. Return the soup to the pan and season with salt, freshly ground peppercorns and lemon juice. Reheat the soup just before serving.
4. Mix together butter and garlic; spread thinly on bread slices and toast them. Cut each toast in triangles or in any other shape.

Serving: Pour hot soup in each soup plate; arrange the cut bread pieces of 1 slice on top; and serve garnished with 1 tbsp cheese.

You may place bread triangles on the bottom of the soup plate and then pour hot soup over.

Cooking time: 40 to 45 minutes.

7.Chickpeas Soup with Pasta

(Pasta e ceci)

This is another variety of thick Italian soups.

You Require:

Boiled chickpeas	2 cups	Bacon diced	¼ cup (opt)
Garlic peeled	3 cloves	Olive oil	4 to 6 tbsp
Short pasta (ditalini)	½ cup	Bay leaf	1 no
Rosemary dried	¼ tsp		
Or			
Fresh sprig	2 no	Water / veg stock	5 cups
Salt-n-pepper	to taste	Parmesan cheese grated to serve with	

Preparation and Cooking:

1 Combine in a deep pan chickpeas, water, rosemary, bay leaf, 2 cloves of garlic and 3 tbsp olive oil; bring to the boiling point and then simmer for 30 to 40 minutes. Remove from fire and discard bay leaf. Puree half of the chickpeas with some liquid from the pan and mix with the remaining chickpeas
2. Meantime when chickpeas are simmering, boil pasta in salted water with 1 tsp cooking oil; drain and keep aside.
3. In remaining oil sauté diced bacon along with remaining garlic until golden brown. Discard garlic. And stir the pork with its oils into the chickpeas mixture.
4. Now add 1 and 1/2 cups of water to the chickpeas and bring it to the boiling point. Add boiled pasta into the soup and check the seasonings. Simmer the soup for 5 minutes and switch off the heat.
5. Stand the soup for 10 to 15 minutes, so that the flavours mingle and the soup develops the texture.

Serving: Serve the soup hot sprinkled with a little grated parmesan, or keep the grated cheese separately for those who want to enrich the dish.

Cooking time: 1 hour.

8. Mushroom Soup with Dry and Fresh Mushrooms

(Zuppa di porcini)

You Require:

Fresh mushrooms	400 gm / 3 cups	Dry mushrooms	1 cup
Olive oil / butter	3 tbsp	Leeks	2 no
Shallots	3 no	Garlic	2 cloves
Thyme dried	½ tsp	Salt and pepper	to taste
Fresh cream	¼ cup	Veg/non-vegetarian stock	6 cups
Fresh thyme for garnishing			

Preparation and Cooking:

1. Soak the dried mushrooms in a bowl of warm water for 30 minutes. Meantime, chop the leeks, shallots and garlic. Chop the fresh mushrooms, too.
2. Lift soaked mushrooms out of water and squeeze properly over the bowl in which they were soaked. Save the liquid to be used later. Chop the mushrooms.
3. Heat fat in a large pan and sauté leeks, shallots and garlic, stirring all the time. Add chopped fresh mushrooms and cook on medium heat for a few minutes. Add stock and bring to the boiling point. Add saved liquid from dry mushrooms too. Add copped dry mushrooms and simmer on low heat for 30 minutes or so. Add salt and pepper also when soup is simmering.

4. Blend three-fourth of the soup in a blender/processor until smooth and put the mixture back in the pan with the remaining soup. Heat the soup. Add cream; check the seasonings and the consistency; add more stock or water if the soup appears too thick.

Serving: Garnish the 'Mushroom Soup' with fresh thyme and serve it hot with any crusty bread.

Cooking time: 50 minutes.

9.Roasted Tomatoes, Pepper and Fresh Basil Soup

(Crema di pomodori pepperoni al basilica)

This appetizing soup is mostly prepared with bread also in it.

You Require:

Tomatoes	1000 gm	Red peppers	2 no
Olive oil	2 tbsp	Garlic peeled	3 cloves
Spring onions	3 no	Cumin	2 tsp
Ground coriander	1 tsp	White bread	2 slices
Balsamic vinegar	1 tbsp	Veg / non-veg stock	5 cup
Salt-n-pepper	to taste	Basil freshly chopped	3 tbsp
Parmesan cheese grated	optional		

Preparation and Cooking:

1. Roast tomatoes and peppers in a hot oven placed in a lightly oiled tray for 25 to 30 minutes or until their skins are charred and blisters appear. Cool, remove the skins and chop.
2. Chop onions, crush garlic; remove the crust from bread and break the slices in tiny pieces.
3. Heat the oil in a saucepan, add garlic and the onion and cook till soft. Add cumin and coriander, stir for a few seconds; add chopped tomatoes-n-peppers and stock; bring the mixture to a boil and simmer for 30 minutes. Add bread, vinegar, half the basil and seasonings; stir and cook further for 5 to 10 minutes.

Serving: Serve it hot garnished with remaining Basil and Parmesan cheese.

Cooking time: 1 hour

10. Pumpkin Soup

(Minestrone di zucca)

You Require:

Pumpkin	1 kg	Butter	3 tbsp
Onion chopped	1 medium	Chicken stock / water	4 cups
Milk	2 cups	Spaghetti broken	1/3 cup

Nutmeg grated	a pinch	Freshly ground pepper	1 tsp or to taste
Salt	to taste		

Parmesan cheese (grated) to serve the soup with

Preparation and Cooking:

1. Clean and cut pumpkin into small pieces.
2. Heat butter; sauté onion in it and then add pumpkin. Stir for 1 minute; add stock / water and cook till pumpkin is soft.
3. Remove from heat; cool a bit and pass through a blender. Return it to the pan; stir in milk, nutmeg, salt and pepper and boil.
4. Par-boil broken spaghetti and stir in the soup. Cook the soup till pasta is done.

   Serving: Add cheese to the ready soup and serve at once.

   Garlic bread or chilli croutons accompany it well.

   Cooking time: 35 minutes.

11. Mutton and Vegetable Stew

(Spezzatino d'agnello)

You Require:

Boneless mutton	500 gm	Small red onions	12 to 15 no
Baby potatoes	15 to 20 no	Cherry tomatoes	12 to 15
Carrots diced	1 cup	Green pepper	1 large
Red pepper	1 small	Yellow pepper	1 small (opt)
Garlic chopped	2 tbsp	Tomato puree	½ cup
Olive oil	¼ cup	Pepper powder	1 tbsp
Italian herbs	2 tsp	Dry white wine	½ cup
Fresh rosemary/ parsley	2 sprigs	Seasoned flour	¼ cup
Bouquet garni		Salt	to taste

Cauliflower / broccoli flowerets from 1 small head

Preparation and Cooking:

1. Preheat the oven to 180 degrees Celsius.
2. Cut boneless lamb in 1 and ½ inch pieces and dredge with flour mixed with salt and pepper. Keep it for 10 minutes.
3. Meantime rub baby potatoes nicely and peel off small onions.
4. Heat oil in a heavy bottomed pan and add meat pieces in two batches and brown them from all sides; remove with a slotted spoon and place in a large casserole.

5. In the same pan sauté garlic; add baby potatoes and small onions and brown them a bit, and put them in the same casserole. Add bouquet garni, parsley or rosemary sprigs, 2 cups of hot mutton stock or water, tomato puree and wine. Cover the casserole with a lid or a piece of aluminum foil and place in the centre of the oven. Cook for 1 and ½ hours.
6. Par-boil cauliflower / broccoli and carrots; cut peppers in squares and keep them ready.
7. After 1 and ½ hours remove the casserole and remove the bag of bouquet garni and parsley sprigs; squeeze the juices of bouquet garni bag into the stew and discard the sprigs.
8. Add prepared vegetables, cherry tomatoes and Italian herbs; add ½ cup water if stew seems very thick and cook it for 30 minutes more in the oven, uncovered.
9. Remove the casserole from oven; and check salt and pepper.

Serving: Serve the stew hot garnished with chopped Parsley and Tabasco. Any kind of bread or the garlic toasts are the best accompaniment.

Variation: Cook the Mutton stew without vegetables. It is just yummy.

Use button Mushrooms instead of boneless mutton.

You may add ¼ tsp of Red chili powder to the cooking stew.

Cooking time: 2 hours.

12.Vegetable Stew

You Require:

Carrots	2 medium	Capsicum	1 large
Green peas shelled	½ cup	Beans chopped	½ cup
Potato cubes	½ cup	Cauliflower (broken into pieces)	1 cup
Tomatoes	500 gm	Garlic chopped fine	1 tbsp
Onion chopped fine	1 small	Olive oil / butter	2 tbsp
Dry red chilli deseeded	1 no	Mixed herbs	1 tsp
Tastemaker cube	1 no (opt)	Corn flour	2 tbsp
Grated cheese	¼ cup	Salt-n-pepper	to taste
Water	4 cups / 800 ml		

Preparation and Cooking:

1. Cut tomatoes and pass through an electric blender; strain and keep ready to be used.
2. Cut carrots and capsicum into small pieces. Dissolve soup cube into ¼ cup water.
3. Heat oil in a deep saucepan and add dry broken chilli; once it turns black remove it with a slotted spoon. Saute onion and garlic in the same oil; add potato, cauliflower and carrot pieces in it and stir on high fire for 1 minute; sprinkle corn flour evenly and stir for a few more seconds. Add tomato contents and water. Increase the flame; bring the mixture to the boiling point and simmer the soup for 30 minutes and check the doneness of potato pieces.

4. Add mixed herbs, chopped capsicum, salt and pepper. Simmer for another 15 minutes. Check the seasonings.
5. Remove from the fire and add half of the cheese.

Serving: Serve the stew hot, garnished with remaining grated cheese and a little chopped coriander. Any bread, melba toast or soup sticks can accompany it.

Cooking time: 1 hour.

13.Spinach and Rice Soup

(minestra di riso e spinaci)

This light and refreshing soup is not only yummy but satisfying too.

You Require:

Rice	½	cup	Veg / chicken stock	4	cups
Red pepper	½	small	Green chilli deseeded	1	small
Garlic paste	1	tsp	Onion	1	small
Olive oil (extra virgin)	2	tbsp	Grated cheese	4	tbsp
Salt	to	taste	Freshly crushed pepper	to	taste
Spinach blanched-n-chopped1 to1 and ½ cup					

Preparation and Cooking:

1. Chop onion, green chilli and red pepper very fine.
2. Heat oil in a large pan and sauté onion chilli and pepper till soft; add rice and stir for 30 seconds; add stock and bring it to the boiling point. Boil it on high for 2 minutes and then simmer for 15 minutes.
3. Add chopped spinach, salt and pepper; simmer for another 10 minutes and check the seasonings.

Serving: Pour soup in individual plates and garnish with 1 tbsp grated cheese each.

Tips: In place of stock 1 soup cube-the taste maker can be dissolved in lukewarm water and used to prepare soup.

If you desire, you may pass spinach through liquidizer and then add to the soup. Taste will be the same but appearance of the soup will change.

Cooking time: 30 minutes.

14. Italian Lentils and Pasta Soup

(lenticchie di pasta)

This hearty soup can also be prepared with green lentils if available.

Recipe is from central Italy.

You Require:

Small variety of lentils	1 cup	Ham chopped	½ cup
Olive oil	¼ cup	Chicken / veg stock	8 cups
Onion chopped fine	1 medium	Carrot chopped fine	1 medium
Celery chopped fine	1 stick	Sage fresh	1 twig
Thyme fresh	1 twig	Small soup pasta	1 and ½ cup
Freshly ground pepper	to taste	Salt	to taste
Parsley fresh	1 twig		

Preparation and Cooking:

1. Soak lentils in fresh water for 3 to 4 hours.
2. Heat oil in a deep pan, sauté the ham; add chopped onion and cook till transparent. Stir in the carrot and celery and cook for 2 to 3 minutes.
3. Drain the lentils and add to the pan. Stir properly to coat them well with oil.
4. Pour in the stock and add herbs. Bring the mixture to the boiling point, lower the heat and simmer for almost 1 hour or until the lentils are tender. Season the soup with salt and pepper. Remove the twigs of sage and thyme and squeeze their juices into the soup bowl.
5. Now add pasta and cook on medium fire until it is done but still crisp.

   Serving: Serve **'Lentils and Pasta Soup'** hot garnished with parsley.

   Cooking time: 1 and ½ hour.

15. Asparagus Soup

(zuppa di asparagus)

Asparagus is a great vegetable with its inherent minerals. Its soup is just ideal to start a light meal. Any bread is the best accompaniment to it.

You Require:

Asparagus	300 gm	Cooking oil	1 tbsp
Onion sliced	1 medium	Garlic chopped	1 clove
Potato cubed	1 no medium	Vegetable stock	600 ml
Spice powder	½ tsp	Salt and pepper	to taste

Preparation and Cooking:

1. Discard the woody ends of asparagus and slice it.
2. Heat oil in a pan; sauté onion in it until soft; add chopped garlic and stir for a few seconds.
3. Add sliced asparagus, potato cubes and vegetable stock. Bring the mixture to the boiling point and simmer till the vegetables are tender. Switch off the fire and cool the veggies slightly.

4. Puree until smooth. Season it with salt, pepper and spice powder. Add ¼ to ½ cup boiled water if the soup seems very thick and check the seasonings once again.

   Serving: Reheat **Asparagus Soup** before serving with any bread or a grilled sandwich.

   Cooking time: 30 minutes.

16. Fish Soup

(ciuppin)

Saffron is a great spice to be used with fish as it helps to cool its heating properties.

You Require:

Firm fillets of white fish	4 no	Olive oil / butter	2 tbsp
Carrot peeled and chopped	1 large	Onion chopped	1 large
Thyme fresh	1 sprig	Garlic peeled	1 clove
Fennel head chopped	1 small	Fish stock / water	800 ml
Saffron	a few strands	Parsley to garnish	2 tbsp
White wine	50 ml		
Or			
Fresh lemon	1 large	Salt-n-pepper	to taste

Preparation and Cooking:

1. Heat oil or butter in a deep pan and sauté the chopped vegetables for 5 minutes or until the vegetables are slightly soft. Take out two tbsp for garnishing to be used later,
2. Add garlic, herbs and seasonings; stir; and add fish stock or water. Bring the mixture to the boiling point and then simmer for 15 minutes; slightly cool the mixture and pass through a sieve.
3. Return the liquid to a pan and heat up. Cut the fish fillet in big chunks and saved vegetables into small pieces; add to the liquid with saffron; simmer for 5 minutes or until the fish is cooked.
4. Lift the fish and divide into 4 bowls. Squeeze lemon juice into the fish stew; add parsley and check for the right taste; adjust seasonings if needed be; and finally pour the stew over fish.

Serving: Serve the soup hot garnished with a little more parsley; and you may add a drop or two of fresh cream too. Crusty bread is an excellent accompaniment to the dish.

Cooking time: Approximately 40 minutes.

17. Minestronne with Rice

(Minestra di riso)

Minestrone can be cooked with any combination of seasonal vegetables; it's a thick soup; though short pasta is added in it, yet it is cooked with rice also.

You Require:

Onion chopped fine	1 large	Leek sliced	1 no
Carrot chopped fine	1 large	Celery stick chopped fine	1 no
Garlic chopped fine	2 cloves	Mushroom sliced	6 to 8 no
OR			
Thyme leaves fresh	1 sprig	Tomatoes peeled and chopped	3 to 4 medium
Green peas shelled	½ cup	Rice brown	½ cup (raw)
Red chilli fresh	1 no	Any beans fresh	½ cup
Olive oil	3 tbsp	Salt-n-pepper	to taste
Stock	7 cups		
Water + soup cube	1or 2 no	Grated parmesan (opt) ¼ cup	
Pine nuts for garnishing	optional	Basil for garnishing	
OR			
Almond slivers			

Preparation and Cooking:

1. Wash and soak rice. Heat up stock / water. Deseed red chilli and chop it.
2. Heat oil in a large-deep pan; sauté onion and leek until transparent; add carrots, celery, chilli and potatoes and cook for a minute or two.
3. Add stock and the herbs; bring them to boiling point and then simmer on medium fire for 10 minutes. Add sliced mushroom.
4. Drain rice and add to the simmering stock; add beans, peas and tomatoes; season with salt and pepper and simmer till rice is tender and soup appears thick.
5. Once it is ready stand the soup for 5 minutes and add cheese.

Serving: Serve the soup hot garnished with roasted pines /almond slivers and fresh chopped basil.

Cooking time: about 35 minutes.

18. Chicken Soup with Vermicelli

(Bordo)

A well flavoured soup made with chicken broth and angle pasta or roasted vermicelli.

You Require:

Chicken cleaned	1 small	Onion sliced	1 large
Olive oil	2 tbsp	Peppercorns	1 tsp
Cinnamon-stick	1 piece of 2"	All spice berries	1 tsp
Bay leaf	1 no	Cloves	6 no
Salt-n pepper	to taste	Vermicelli	½ cup
Water	6 cups	Basil leaves for garnishing	
Lemon wedges to be served (opt)			

Preparation and Cooking:

1. Heat oil in a deep pan, sauté onion; add whole spices and chicken; stir for 2 to 3 minutes and then add water; bring the mixture to the boiling point, reduce the heat and simmer the soup for 45 minutes or till chicken is soft.
2. Lift the chicken out of the stock with a slotting spoon and cool slightly.
3. Strain the stock and keep aside. Discard onion mixture.
4. Roast vermicelli in a non-stick pan till golden in colour.
5. Take out the flesh from the chicken breasts and cut into pieces of desired size.
6. Return the pan of chicken stock to fire; add roasted vermicelli; season it with salt and pepper and add chicken pieces. Simmer once.

Serving: Serve it garnished with fresh basil leaves and squeeze lemon juice according to your taste. Serve the crusty bread and a vegetable salad with it.

Variation: You may add finely chopped vegetables and a little grated cheese to make more whole-some.

Cooking time: 1 hour.

19. Barley-Vegetable Soup

(Minestrone d' orzo)

This nourishing thick soup originates from Italy's mountainous region and served with bread makes a full meal.

You Require:

Chicken/ meat broth	5 cups	Olive oil	2 tbsp
Or			
Veg stock + 1 soup cube		Pearl barley	½ cup
Onion chopped	1 medium	Carrot chopped	1 medium
Celery stick copped fine	1 no	Leek sliced	½ no
Potato chopped fine	1 no small	Ham / chicken diced	¼ cup

Rosemary fresh	1 sprig		
Or			
Rosemary dry	¼ tsp	Fresh parsley chopped	2 tbsp
Salt-n-pepper	to taste		
Parmesan cheese grated to serve along (opt)			

Preparation and Cooking:

1. Soak barley for 4 hours.
2. Drain it and put in a pan with stock; bring to the boiling point and then simmer for 30 minutes.
3. Heat oil in another pan; sauté all the vegetables and add into the simmering barley. Add rosemary and ham / chicken and cook while simmering until the vegetables are soft.
4. Season it with salt and freshly ground pepper to your taste. Serve with cheese if using.

Note: You may not add cheese to this excellent soup cooked with ham, but add it to the vegetarian version for additional taste.

Serving: Serve the soup hot garnished with parsley and serve crusty bread as an accompaniment.

Cooking time: 1 hour 15 minues.

20. Chicken Stew

(Stew di pollo)

Another excellent - satisfying soup, a meal in itself which should be served for light lunch/ dinner; and it is sumptuous.

You Require:

Chicken breasts (cut into 4 pieces)	2 no		
Potato cut into cubes	1 medium	Carrot cut into cubes	1 large
Onion chopped	1 large	Fresh beans cut	½ cup
Cauliflower/broccoli florets	1 cup	Courgette (yellow) cubed	½ cup
Celery stick chopped	1 no	Tomato skinned-chopped	1 large
Leek sliced	½ no	Fresh thyme	1 sprig
Fresh sage	1 sprig	Garlic paste	1 tsp
Corn flour	1 tbsp	Butter / olive oil	2 tbsp
Bay leaf	1 no	Water	6 cups
Fresh peppercorns	1 tbsp	Seasonings	to taste
Fresh chopped parsley to serve		Roasted almond flakes to serve(opt)	

Preparation and Cooking:

1. Heat the butter/oil in large sauce pan; sauté onion, leek and other chopped vegetables, except tomato, in the same order; add garlic paste; sprinkle corn flour over the vegetables and cook on high fire for a few seconds. Add water and bring the mixture to the boiling point.
2. Add sprigs of herbs and chicken breasts into the mixture; lower the heat and simmer for 30 minutes or until chicken is tender enough to be eaten.
3. Add chopped tomato and fresh peppercorns; cook for 5 minutes and remove from heat. Remove bay leaf and sprigs of herbs. Squeeze the juice into the soup.
4. Season the soup to your choice. Add parsley and check the consistency of thickness.

Serving: Lift the chicken breasts with a slotted spoon. Divide the soup in 4 bowls; top it with 1 piece of chicken breast each; garnish with roasted almonds and serve it hot.

You may serve melba toast with it.

Variation: If you do not want vegetable pieces along with chicken in the stew, you may mash the vegetables after lifting chicken and pass through a coarse sieve before serving. You may cut chicken breasts in edible pieces.

Cooking time: 45 minutes.

❐

Spinach and Rice Soup

Salads / Insalata

Roasted Peppers and Tomato Salad

Mushroom Spinach & Baked Beans Salad

Sweet & Sour Onion Salad

Roasted Potatoes Salad

Salad Italiana

Tomato, Mozzarella & Basil Salad

Tuna and Blackeyed Bean Salad

Whole Wheat Pasta Salad

Roasted Chicken Salad

Peppers and Pasta Salad

Crouton Salad

Chickpeas Salad with Shallots & Black Olives

Roasted Peppers and Tomato Salad

Salads / Insalata

The salads from Italy are numerous. The list of irresistible and delicious salads is pretty long; and the combinations of marvellous crunchy salads are endless as there is no dearth of fresh vegetables in Italy. Often we find the combination of roasted ingredients tossed with crisp green leaves (salad leaves). The variety of salad leaves such as Dandelion leaves, Radicchio (round red leafed chicory), Rocket (the hot pungent salad leaf) and Corn-salad leaves etc are not available in India. Now, with globalization, some times you see such rare ingredients in the super markets of Malls. In our recipes, mostly we have used lettuce leaves, commonly available in India.

1. Peppers and Pasta Salad

(Insalata di pepperoni e pasta)

You Require:

Cut macaroni	200	gm	Green pepper roasted	1	no
Carrots	2	no	Red pepper roasted	1	no
Cabbage	8	leaves	Mayonnaise	½	cup
Mustard sauce	¼	cup	Chili-garlic sauce	1	tbsp
Tomato sauce	¼ cup	(opt)	Fresh cream	¼ cup	(opt)
Salt (if required)	to	taste	Cucumber	1	Small

Preparation and Cooking:

1. Boil enough water in a big bowl and add macaroni, 1 tsp salt and 1 tsp oil. Cook till almost done and drain.
2. Remove and drain water and run under the tap. Smear with a little olive oil. Keep th em covered peel the peppers.
3. Chop peppers and carrots in matchstick fashion.
4. Remove the spine of cabbage leaves, roll them tightly and shred fine. Soak cabbage in cold water for 30 minutes. Drain and keep cool under refrigeration.
5. For greener effect slice cucumber thinly without peeling it.

Assembling: Mix red and green pepper and macaroni in a bowl; pour all the sauces over and toss once or twice. Or mix gently with a light hand and refrigerate salad at least for 30 minutes before serving.

Serving: Arrange cucumber and carrot on a large platter; lay cooled cabbage on top and then place the pasta salad in the centre.

Cooking time: 22 minutes.

2. Sweet and Sour Onion Salad

(Insalata di cipolle in agrodolce)

You Require:

Baby onions (red)	500 gm	Wine vinegar	¼ cup
Olive oil	3 tbsp	Castor sugar	3 tbsp
Tomato puree	3 tbsp	Bay leaf	1 no
Parsley	2 sprigs	Raisins	¼ cup
Freshly ground pepper	1 tsp	Salt	to taste

Preparation and Cooking:

1. Put the onion in a micro safe bowl; add wine vinegar, olive oil, sugar, tomato puree, parsley, raisins, salt and pepper.
2. Add 1 cup of water and cook for 15 minutes, uncovered, first 5 minutes on HIGH and next 10 minutes on micro MEDIUM.
3. Remove the bay leaf and parsley.
4. Check the seasoning.

Serving: Serve this pungent salad at room temperature.

Cooking time:15 minutes.

3. Salad Italiana

(Insalata Italiana)

You Require:

Macaroni (Gremiti)	1 cup	Potatoes	2 large
Carrots	2 large	Cucumbers	2 medium
Green peas shelled	½ cup	Chives dry	1 tsp
Beans cut into 1" pieces	1 cup	Olive oil	1 tbsp
Italian dressing (Readymade)			
Or			
Tomato sauce	½ cup	Worcestershire sauce	1 tbsp
Cinnamon powder	½ tsp	White pepper powder	1 tsp
Salt	to taste	Cheese grated	¼ cup (opt)

Preparation and Cooking:

1. Boil 5 cups of water with 1tsp salt and oil each; put in gremiti pasta and boil on full flame till soft. Drain and run under tap water to stop further cooking. Smear it with 1 tsp olive oil and keep covered. It will take almost 15 minutes to complete the process of cooling.

2. Meantime peel and cut potatoes, carrots and cucumbers into cubes.
3. Place potatoes in the steaming basket of a microwave and steam for 5 minutes on HIGH and stand it for 5 minutes. Remove.
4. Steam beans, carrots and green peas, too, for 3 minutes on micro HIGH; remove immediately and place under tap water to retain the crunchiness and the colour of the vegetables.
5. Combine boiled pasta, potato, carrots, bean, green peas and cucumbers in a serving bowl; cover and chill.
6. Combine all the ingredients of dressing and beat well, chill it for 15 minutes and mix it with boiled vegetables and pasta. Keep it under refrigeration till served.

Serving: Serve it in a fancy salad bowl or line a platter with salad leaves and pile chilled salad on top. Sprinkle it with chives.

Variation: Reduce the quantity of vegetables to half and add 1 and ½ cup cooked and shredded chicken to the salad.

Cooking time: 30 minutes and chilling time extra.

4.Chickpeas Salad with Shallots and Black Olives

(Ceci, chipolline e olive in insalata)

You Require:

Chickpeas soaked and boiled

Or

Canned chickpeas	450 gm	Shallots	15 to 20 no
Tomatoes	2 no	Black olives stoned	10 to 12 no
Onion sliced	1 medium	Parsley chopped	2 tbsp
		Or	
		Coriander chopped	3 tbsp

For dressing:

Wine vinegar	3 tbsp	Olive oil	3 to 4 tbsp
Freshly ground pepper	to taste	Salt	to taste
Oregano dry	½ tsp	Preserved red/green peppercorns (opt)	
Hard boiled eggs for garnishing	3 no		

Preparation:

1. Clean and wash shallots.
2. Cut tomatoes into small cubes.
3. Slice olives into rings.

4. Place chickpeas in a mixing bowl; add the chopped tomatoes, olives, onion and cleaned shallots and mix lightly.
5. In a small bowl, mix together all the ingredients for dressing thoroughly and pour over chickpeas mixture. Sprinkle chopped parsley over the salad.
6. Toss the salad and let it stand for 1 hour before serving, so that all the flavours blend well with the chickpeas and vegetables.

Serving: Transfer the salad in a serving dish. Garnish it with egg halves or wedges just before serving.

Variation: Instead of chickpeas kidney beans / green chickpeas or any other canned beans can be used for this preparation. Spring onions can be substituted in this salad.

Preparation time: 20 to 25 minutes.

5. Whole-Wheat Pasta Salad

(Insalta di pasta integrale)

You Require:

Whole wheat pasta (conchiglie rigate)	2 cups un-boiled		
Olive oil	2 tbsp	Spring onions sliced	3 no
Red, green yellow peppers	1 each	Broccoli / cauliflower	1small head
Carrots cubed	1 large	Green peas shelled	½ cup
Celery sticks chopped	2 no	Cherry tomatoes halved	10 no
Olives black / green sliced	10 no	Chicken salamis	8 to10 no (opt)
For the Dressing:			
Wine vinegar	3 tbsp	Olive oil	3 tbsp
Mustard powder	2 tsp	Pepper powder	2 tsp
Sesame seeds	1 tbsp	Cheddar cheese grated	½ cup
Fresh herbs chopped (parsley, basil, thyme etc)	¼ cup	Salt	to taste
Or			
Mixed herbs dried	1 tsp		

Preparation and Cooking:

1. Boil pasta in boiling salted water in a large pan till done and drain. Rinse with cold water; drain well; smear it with 2 tbsp olive oil and keep aside.
2. Roast peppers; clean and chop them.

3. Combine carrots, peas and broccoli / cauliflower broken in flowerets and either steam in a microwave for 3 to 4 minutes or lightly blanch in boiling water; immediately drain and rinse under tap water to retain the colour. Combine with boiled pasta in a large mixing bowl.
4. Combine all the ingredients for dressing in a small bowl except cheese and herbs and mix well. Pour the dressing over pasta mixture and toss. Check the seasonings and adjust.
5. Add cheese and herbs and mix lightly. Add thinly sliced salamis if you are using them. Cover it with foil and let it stand for 30 minutes before serving.

Serving: Garnish with additional basil and serve at room temperature with a light soup.

This dish of whole-wheat pasta is a meal in itself, so other accompaniments of the meal can be lighter.

Tips: Pasta can be boiled before hand; vegetables can be steamed earlier and dressing can be prepared and final mixing can be done 30 minutes before a meal.

Cooking time: 1 hour.

6. Roasted Potato Salad

(Insalata di patate arrostiti)

You Require:

Potatoes	6 no	medium	Roasted tomatoes	3 no	medium
Roasted pepper (g)	1	large	Salad leaves	8	no
Celery-stick	1	no	Fresh peppercorns	1	tbsp
Olive oil	2 to 3	tbsp	Lemon-pepper	½	tsp
Oregano dry	1	tsp	Table vinegar	1	tbsp
Salt to taste					

Preparation and Cooking:

1. Preheat the oven to 180 degrees Celsius.
2. Peel and cut potatoes in ½ -cubes; smear with 2 tbsp olive oil and roast in hot oven for 40 to 45 minutes. Stir twice in between.
3. Soak salad leaves in cold water.
4. Roast tomatoes and pepper; remove the skin and cut into cubes.
5. Chop celery fine. Break the salad leaves.
6. Remove potatoes from oven and transfer to a serving bowl; add all the chopped vegetables and stir lightly.
7. Combine vinegar, remaining oil, lemon-pepper and oregano; pour over roasted vegetables and toss. Add salt according to taste and mix once again. Chill for 30 minutes at least.

Serving: Serve on the bed of lettuce with salad sticks.

Cooking time: 1 hour.

7.Mushrooms, Spinach and Baked Beans Salad

(Insalata di porcini,spinaci e borlotti beans)

One of the rare seasonal salads which is relished everywhere.

You Require:

Mushrooms sliced	2 cups	Fresh Spinach chopped	
Or			
Baby spinach	2 cups	Baked-beans (drained)	1 cup
Spring onions sliced	½ cup	Cucumber cubed	1 cup
Grated cheese	¼ cup (opt)	Honey-lemon dressing	½ cup
Fresh Spinach chopped	2 cups		

Preparation for Honey-lemon dressing:

Combine the following ingredients together and chill before use:

Balsamic vinegar – ¼ cup, fresh lemon-juice -2 tbsp, honey -2 tbsp, Olive oil -1 tbsp, pepper powder – 2 tsp, salt to taste (opt)

Assembly: Take a platter, spread spinach nicely; mix the remaining ingredients in a bowl and pour the dressing over Stir lightly and arrange on the spinach bed.

Serving: Serve the salad cold.

Tips: Soak spinach leaves in cold water for 30 minutes before chopping them. Drain, pat them dry with a kitchen towel, roll 4 to 5 leaves together and chop them fine. Store in a refrigerator till used.

Preparation time: 15 to 20 minutes.

8. Roasted Peppers and Tomato Salad

A popular Italian salad relished anytime all over the country.

You Require:

Peppers (red & green)	2 each	Tomatoes large	2 no
Sun dried tomatoes	2 tbsp	Sliced Garlic	2 tbsp
Spring onions	3 no	Pine nuts	2 tbsp
Basil (fresh)	2 tbsp	Balsamic vinegar	2 tbsp
Lemon juice	1 tbsp	Olive oil	2 tbsp
Salt-n-pepper	to taste	Salad leaves	6 no
		Capers	1 tbsp

Preparation and Cooking:

1. Soak sun dried tomatoes in lukewarm water. Soak salad leaves in cold water.

2. Roast peppers and place them in a plastic bag for 10 to 15 minutes and then peel them. Roast and peel tomatoes, too. Chop peppers and tomatoes in the same fashion.Slice spring onions with tender greens. Lift the sun dried tomatoes from water and slice them.
3. Roast pine nuts on medium heat in a pan. Roast garlic too in the same pan with a few drops olive oil in it.
4. Combine all the vegetables in the serving bowl or in a salad plate.
5. Combine olive oil, vinegar and lemon juice in a small bowl. Add 1 tsp salt and ½ tsp pepper powder. Mix it well and add to the bowl with peppers and other vegetables.
6. Break salad leaves into pieces and mix with the vegetables. Add basil, capers and garlic to the salad. Mix lightly.

   Serving: Serve the salad at room temperature garnished with pine nuts and basil leaves.

   Cooking time: 40 to 45 minutes.

9. Tuna and Black Eyed Bean Salad

(Tonno e black eyed beans in insalata)

You Require:

Tuna fish tinned	1 no	Black-eyed beans	1 cup dry
Olive oil	3 tbsp	Lemon juice	2 tbsp
Lemon pepper	1 tsp (opt)	Spring onions sliced	3 no
Green chilli chopped	1 no	Red peppercorns	1 tbsp
Salt-n-pepper	to taste	Parsley chopped	2 tbsp
Red Pepper	½ (opt)		

Preparation and Cooking:

1. Wash and soak beans for 1 hour; cook in a pressure cooker with 3 cups water for 15 minutes and strain. Or cook in a pan with 1 cup extra water , partially covered, till done. Strain. Put in a salad bowl. Save the liquid. You can use it for some gravy or soup.
2. Combine together olive oil, lemon juice, salt and pepper and mix it well. Pour it over boiled beans and mix lightly. Add spring onions, green chillies, pepper and red peppercorns; toss well. Sprinkle lemon pepper and parsley.
3. Take out the tuna fish flakes; separate with a fork and lightly mix with beans mixture. Cover with cling wrap or foil and cool under refrigeration at least for 1 hour.

   Serving: Serve the salad cold with thin toasts and a light soup at any meal.

   Cooking time: 45 minutes.

10.Roasted Chicken Salad

(Insalata di pollo arrostiti)

You Require:

Roasted chicken breasts	2 no	Shallots	1 cup
Black olives halved	½ cup	Mushrooms quartered	1 cup
Parsley chopped	2 tbsp	Cucumber with skin diced	1 no medium
Cherry tomatoes halved	½ cup	Celery sticks sliced	2 no
Lemon-juice	2 tbsp	Mustard sauce	2 tbsp heaped
Extra virgin olive oil	2 tbsp	Lettuce	1 head
Salt and pepper	to taste		

Preparation:

1. Soak salad leaves in cold water for 30 minutes to achieve crispness. Break half the leaves in small pieces.
2. Meantime, slice roasted chicken in bite sized pieces and combine with olives, shallots, mushrooms, cucumber, celery, cherry tomatoes and half of parsley. Toss well.
3. Mix together olive oil, lemon juice, mustard sauce, salt and pepper; pour it over chicken and vegetables and mix with a light hand.
4. Add broken salad leaves; cover and chill for 30 minutes before serving.

Serving: Line a platter with remaining salad leaves and pile up the chicken salad in the centre. Garnish it with remaining parsley and serve immediately.

Preparation time: 40 minutes.

11.Croutons Salad

You Require:

Extra virgin olive oil	3 tbsp	Balsamic vinegar	½ cup
Salt and pepper	to taste	Sugar	1 tsp
Lettuce	6 leaves	Bread slices	4 to 5no
Tomatoes	2 large	Spring onions	3 no
Cucumber	2 small	Green pepper	1 no
Capers (opt)	2 tbsp		

Preparation:

1. Cut bread into small squares and smear with 1 tbsp oil and a pinch of salt. Either roast them on the turn table of a microwave for 4 minutes on HIGH ie 100% power, stirring once in between, or in a hot oven till done. Remove from the oven and cool.

2. Mix vinegar, olive oil, salt, pepper and sugar in a bottle nicely and refrigerate the dressing.
3. Soak lettuce in cold water. Cut cucumber, tomatoes, spring onion and pepper into ½ inch pieces and combine. Break lettuce into edible pieces and add to the vegetables.
4. Combine vegetables and bread croutons in a large bowl and pour dressing over them. Toss the salad and stand it for 30 minutes in a cool place. Toss once again before serving.

   Serving: Serve it as a starter or as a first course.

   Preparation time: 30 minutes.

❐

Tangy Broccoli Salad

FROM THE MARKETS OF ITALY

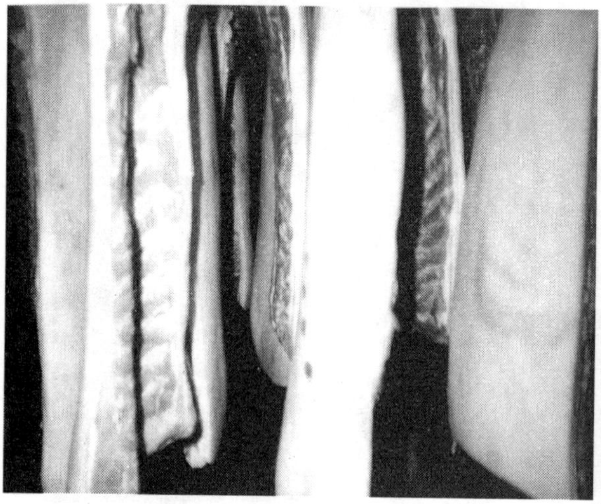

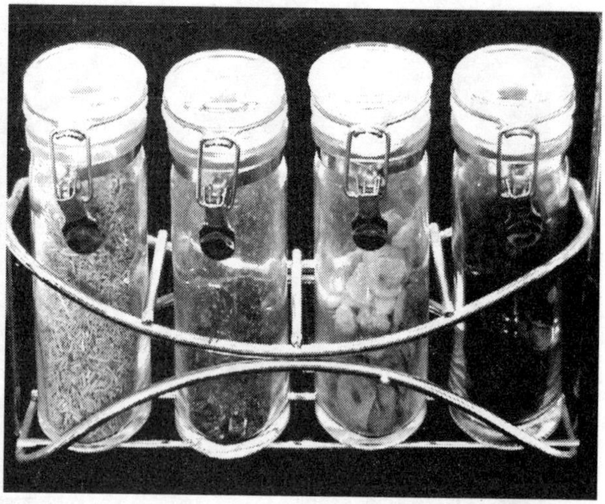

Antipasti / Starters

Prawns on Skewers

Potato Gnocchi

Frittata with Spinach

Roast Mushroom Caps

Bruschetta with Tomato

Eggplant Fritters

Risotto Cake

Potato Pizza

Bread, Mozzarella & Tomato Skewers

Calzone

Fried Pizza Patties

Italian Meat Balls

Tomato Tart

Chickpeas Patties with Yogurt Dip

Baked Eggs with Tomatoes

Batter Fried Prawns

Chili Tomato Cheese Toasts

Ham Sandwich

Grilled Fish Kebabs

Onion-Jalapeno Flavoured Cheddar Cheese Display

Melting Mozzarella Snack

Italian Cheese and Rice Balls

Vegetables with Olive Oil Dip

Eggplant Walnut Dip

Chicken Breasts Stuffed with Cheese and Ham

Crostini

Tomato, Mozzarella and Basil Salad

Antipasti / Starters

Antipasti means 'before the meal', and no Italian meal starts without it. Italian antipasti are tasty and appetizing, appeasing to the eye and light on stomach. Vegetables, fish and salads which fall in this category are known not only for their freshness and lightness but also for their endless pleasing colours.

1. Tomatoes, Mozzarella and Basil Salad

(Insalata caprese) Insalata di pomodori,mozzarella e basillico

This is one of the simplest and very popular Italian salads. In Italy it is considered rather patriotic as the three colours of the ingredients (vegetable, cheese and herb) used in preparation represent the colours of Italy's national flag.

You Require:

Large tomatoes	4 no	Mozzarella cheese	150 gm
Basil leaves	8 to 10 no	Olive oil	3 to 4 tbsp
Freshly ground pepper		Salt	to taste

Preparation:

1. Wash; dry tomatoes and cut them into slices.
2. Cut mozzarella also into thick slices.
3. Arrange them alternately into a circle and decorate with basil leaves.
4. Sprinkle with olive oil and salt. You may sprinkle pepper over the salad or pass it on separately to be used according to the diner's choice.

Serving: Serve it as antipasti.

Preparation time: 15 to 20 minutes.

2.Crostini

Crostini, the small pieces of toasted bread are made with various toppings and are served as one of the antipasti with hot or cold drinks. They are an excellent accompaniment to soups also. They can be topped with cheese, seafood or meats.

You Require:

Day old bread	6 slices	Roasted red pepper	½ no
Cheese slices	6 no		
Or			
Thinly sliced cheddar cheese		Pepper	to taste

Preparation and Baking:

1. Cut the bread slices into any shape of your choice. It may be circle, triangle, oval, heart shape or a star.
2. Preheat the oven to 190 degrees Celsius.
3. Cut cheese slices also in the same shape.
4. Place a cut slice of cheese on the bread.
5. Cut small roundels of pepper too. You may cut any other fancy shape and place on top of the cheese.
6. Sprinkle a little pepper on top of each piece.
7. Place in the greased baking tray and bake for 10 minutes or till cheese melts

   Serving: Serve Crostini hot from the oven or at room temperature.

Note: If you increase the number of bread slices, increase the quantity of cheese also. If you are using cheese slices, after cutting the required number of shapes from them, the trimmings can be used anywhere in baking or cooking omelets etc.

Cooking time: 20 minutes.

3. Potato Gnocchi

(Gnocchi di patate)

Gnocchi is different than pasta but more like dumplings. They are made with semolina, flour, potato or ricotta and spinach. They may be shaped like elongated shells, ovals, cylinders or flat discs. They should be made extremely light that almost melts in mouth. The best known gnocchi are from northern Italy made with potatoes and a little flour.

You Require:

Potatoes	500 gm	Flour	100 gm
Egg	1 large	Salt	2 tsp
Pepper	1 tsp	Tomato sauce for dressing	

Preparation and Cooking:

1. Boil potatoes and mash them; cool and add egg and mix.
2. Sprinkle flour, 1 tsp salt and pepper till you have smooth sticky dough that forms a ball.
3. Turn out the dough on to a floured surface and knead for 3 minutes until smooth and soft. Cut the dough into 4 to 5 equal parts. With the help of flour roll each portion into a sausage shape and slice it into 2" pieces. Hold a fork in the one hand and with other press each piece on the tines of the fork just hard enough to make ridge impression, then slide downwards.
4. Heat enough water in a large pan / kadai with 1 tsp salt in it, bring it to the boiling point and lower the heat. Poach the shaped gnocchi in batches in this lightly salted water which

is barely simmering for 5 to 7 minutes. Gnocchi will rise to the surface; drain them with a perforated / slotted spoon. Keep them warm in a casserole while you are cooking rest of the gnocchi.

Serving: Serve Gnocchi as a first course.

Tips: Gnocchi can be served like any pasta as a first course/ in clear soup as dumplings or as a side dish to the main course with any sauce or just dredged with freshly grated Parmesan cheese.

Cooking time: 35 to 40 minutes.

4.Gnocchi Alla Romana

You Require:

Semolina	200 gm / 1 cup	Milk	3 and ½ cup
Parmesan cheese grated	70 gm	Eggs	2 no
Yolk of the egg	1 no	Butter	50 gm / 3 and ½ tbsp
Nutmeg	a pinch	Salt-n-pepper	to taste

Preparation and Cooking:

1. Boil milk and reduce the heat; season it with salt, pepper and grated nutmeg; and add semolina slowly in a steady stream. Cook it, stirring constantly for almost 15 minutes, until the mixture is very thick.
2. Remove from the heat and add half of the cheese and 2 beaten eggs. Mix well.
3. Pour the mixture into a greased baking tray to a thickness of about ½ inch. Or spread the mixture over a greased platform and leave it to cool thoroughly, then cut into 1 and ½ inch discs with a pastry cutter.
4. Preheat the oven to 220 degrees Celsius.
5. Grease a baking dish with butter and layer the semolina discs in it dotting each layer with melted butter and sprinkling of Parmesan cheese.
6. Bake the gnocchi in hot oven for 15 minutes or so, until browned on top.

Serving: Serve it hot with Tomato sauce

Cooking time: 35 minutes and cooling time extra.

5. Frittata with Spinach

(Frittata con spinaci)

In Italy, frittata is often used as a sandwich filling. It can be used as an antipasti too.

You Require:

Eggs	8 eggs	Spinach cooked	1 cup
Olive oil	3 tbsp	Spring onions with greens	3 no

Garlic	2 cloves	Ham cut into small pieces	½ cup (opt)
Salt-n- pepper	to taste		

Preparation and Cooking:

1. Squeeze cooked spinach and chop it fine. Chop spring onions with their greens too fine. Chop or crush garlic.
2. Heat half the oil and sauté spring onions in it. Add garlic and ham; stir fry for a few seconds or till golden. Add spinach and cook for a few seconds, so that it is warm enough; season with salt and freshly ground pepper and remove from the pan. Clean the pan with paper napkin.
3. Beat eggs with 2 tbsp water and add the spinach mixture to it.
4. Heat the remaining oil and spread over the pan properly; lower the heat and pour egg mixture in it. Keep stirring over the medium heat till the eggs start setting and the bottom turns golden.
5. Take a large plate and place it upside down over the pan; hold the pan firmly and turn it to slide the frittata into the plate carefully. Slide the frittata back into the pan and cook the second side also for 2 to 3 minutes or till it turns golden. Remove.

Note: For fancy cooking, you may prepare small individual frittatas.

Serving: Cut the frittata into wedges and serve it either warm or at room temperature. You may cut it into long strips and serve with any sauce.

Variations:

a. You may serve sliced frittata as a salad.

b. You may cook frittata with leftover pasta.

c. You may cook it with sun dried tomatoes (soaked and sliced) or thick tomato sauce and cheese.

d. You may cook it with leftover minced meat or roasted-shredded chicken.

Cooking time: 15 to 20 minutes.

6. Eggplant Fritters

(Frittelle di melanzane)

This vegetarian supper dish is not only superb in preparation but also delicious in taste.

You Require:

Large eggplant	1 no	Egg	1 no
Olive oil	2 tbsp	Garlic crushed	2 cloves
Bread crumbs fresh	¼ cup	Parsley chopped	¼ cup
Parmesan cheese grated	1 cup	Feta / cottage cheese crumbled	1 cup

Flour	¼ cup	Freshly crushed peppercorns	2 to 3 tsp
Cooking oil for frying			
To serve with:			
Hung curd	1 cup	Chilli flakes	as much required
Cumin seeds roasted	1 pinch		

Preparation and Cooking:

1. Preheat the oven to 200 degrees Celsius.
2. Combine hung curd, chilli flakes and roasted cumin seeds in a bowl and season it lightly with salt. Keep it under refrigeration till used.
3. Cut eggplant in thin slices; brush slices with olive oil; place them in a baking tray and bake for 15 to 20 minutes.
4. Chop the slices thinly and place them in a large mixing bowl. Add egg, garlic, parsley, breadcrumbs, parmesan and feta cheese and mix well. Season with salt and crushed pepper and let it stand for 15 minutes.
5. Divide the mixture into 8 to10 parts; if the mixture is too wet. Add ½ cup more breadcrumbs and mix again. Form the balls and flatten slightly to give shape.
6. Season flour with salt and pepper and spread in a plate. Now roll the shaped balls in flour coating them well; shake off excess flour.
7. Heat oil for shallow frying and fry them in batches. Cook them from both sides, turning after 1 minute or till golden brown. Drain them on kitchen oil absorbent paper.

   Serving: Serve the Eggplant Fritters with curd mixture.

   Cooking time: 1 hour.

7. Bread, Mozzarella and Tomato Skewers

(Spiedini alla romana)

A salad of oven baked bread squares, mozzarella and tomato pieces, threaded on skewers along with fresh basil, make excellent starters.

You Require:

White bread	8 slices	Mozzarella cheese	200 gm
Tomatoes	3 no medium	Olive oil	2 tbsp
Salt-n-pepper	to taste	Fresh basil leaves	½ cup

Preparation and Cooking:

1. Preheat the oven to 200 degree Celsius.
2. Soak the wooden skewers in cold water for some time to prevent from scorching.
3. Cut mozzarella cheese into ¼ inch thick squares to match the size of the bread.

4. Cut tomato into 4 parts; remove the seeds and cut further each part into two.
5. Remove the crust from the bread slices and cut into squares. Arrange on baking tray and brush them with olive oil. Bake them until bread is golden in colour. Remove from the oven.
6. Arrange skewers, starting each with a piece of bread, then mozzarella topped with a tomato and a basil leaf. Repeat the process once again. Thus, finish arranging all the skewers and sprinkle with salt and pepper. Brush lightly with remaining oil and place on the baking tray. Bake for 10 to 15 minutes or grill in batches until the cheese starts to meeting.

   Serving: Garnish with fresh Basil leaves and serve.

   Cooking time: 30 minutes.

8.Italian Cheese and Rice Balls

(Suppli al telefono)

These rice and cheese balls are actually rice croquettes that contain mozzarella cheese. After frying, cheese melts into strings and start resembling telephone wires.

You Require:

Cold cooked risotto / rice	2 to 3 cups	Ham	50 gm
Eggs	2 no	Mozzarella	120 gm
Salt-n-pepper to season		Dry bread crumbs to coat	
Oil for deep frying			

Preparation and Cooking:

1. Cut ham into tiny cubes and mozzarella also into ¼ inch pieces.
2. Beat eggs and mix with cold rice; season rice with salt and pepper powder nicely. Form the balls out of this mixture and stuff with ham and diced cheese and roll again.
3. Spread the breadcrumbs in a plate and coat rice balls with crumbs.
4. Heat oil in a frying pan, deep fry the balls in it one by one till golden brown and drain on kitchen paper.

   Serving: Serve the balls hot with any sauce.

   Cooking time: 35 to 40 minutes.

9. Cherry Tomatoes with Pesto

(pomodorini con pesto)

Stuffed cherry tomatoes make an excellent starter for any gathering.

You Require:

Cherry tomatoes	8 no	Cheese grated	½ cup
(parmesan / amul)			

Salt-n-pepper	to taste	Pesto sauce	½ cup
For Pesto sauce:			
Pine nuts	1/3rd cup	Basil leaves	¾ cup
Garlic	4 to 5 cloves	Olive oil	¼ cup
Freshly crushed pepper	1 tsp	Salt	1 tsp
Fresh basil for garnishing			

Preparation and Cooking:

1. Wash and dry the tomatoes with kitchen napkin.
2. Slice off the tops of the tomatoes; scoop out carefully either with a peeler or a small spoon and place the tomatoes upside down on a cake cooling rack, so that all the juice drains out. Collect the tomato pulp and save it under refrigeration for any sauce or a soup.
3. Make pesto sauce: Combine the basil, garlic, pine-nuts, olive oil and seasonings in a blender / food processor and blend until smooth. Remove the sauce in a bowl and add cheese. Mix well and adjust the salt and pepper.
4. Stuff the tomatoes: Use a small spoon to fill pesto in the tomatoes and chill the dish for 1 hour before serving.

Serving: Serve the Cherry Tomatoes as a tasty appetizer with drinks, or serve the dish as a part of the meal.

Tips: Pesto sauce can be made in advance and frozen in small containers, but it should be allowed to thaw properly before use.

Preparation time: 45 minutes to 1 hour.

10. Potato Pizza

You Require:

Potatoes	1 kg	Extra virgin oil	1/3 cup
Garlic	2 cloves	Tomatoes	2 large
Capers	2 tbsp		
Or			
Olives sliced	2 tbsp	Anchovy fillets chopped	opt

Preparation and Cooking:

1. Peel and boil potatoes; mash them when still warm; add 2 tbsp of olive oil and mix well. Keep it aside.
2. Chop garlic and tomatoes.
3. Heat 2 tbsp of oil in a pan; sauté garlic and tomatoes and cook over medium heat till tomatoes are soft and dry.

4. Preheat the oven to moderate heat. Oil a shallow dish for baking. Spread half of the mashed potatoes into the dish; cover with the tomato mixture; dot with capers / olives and anchovy and finally spread the rest of the potatoes in a layer covering the filling properly.
5. Brush the top with remaining oil and bake in the hot oven for 30 to 35 minutes or until the top is golden.

Serving: Serve it hot with clear soup and a salad.

Cooking time: 1 hour.

11. Eggplant-Walnut Dip

You Require:

Eggplant	1 medium	Walnut broken	½ cup to ¾ cup
Green chillies	2 no	Garlic roasted chopped	1 tbsp heaped
Coriander chopped	¼ cup	Extra virgin olive oil	¼ cup
Lemon juice	1 tbsp	White pepper powder	¼ tsp
Salt	to taste		

Preparation and Cooking:

1. Roast eggplant directly on the flame till its skin is completely charred; remove the skin and roughly chop the flesh.
2. Coarsely ground the walnut meat.
3. Place roasted eggplant, walnut powder, garlic and green chillies in a blender; blend on slow speed adding olive oil spoon by spoon; add lemon juice and seasonings; and churn once more.
4. Remove in a bowl; check the seasonings and mix with coriander.
5. Cover and refrigerate till in use.

Serving: Serve it along with any chips, par-boiled vegetables or any other starter.

Cooking time: 30 minutes.

12. Roast Mushroom Caps

(Funghi arrosti)

Italians enjoy a variety of mushrooms and even hunt for edible wild variety. They cook them in various forms, as a vegetable, in soups, salads, sauces, as a filling and in combination of meats. Their truffles are converted into the edible scented oil and just a drop of it enhances the flavour of sauces, salads and pastas.

You Require:

Large mushroom caps	8 no	Garlic chopped fine	4 cloves

Celery stick chopped fine	½ no (opt)	Salt-n-pepper	to taste
Parsley chopped	½ cup		
Or			
Fresh coriander chopped			
Extra virgin olive oil for sprinkling			

Preparation and Cooking:

1. Preheat oven for 200 degrees Celsius.
2. Wash and dry mushrooms with a kitchen towel; remove the stems (do not discard them) and with a peeler, carefully, make the cavity of each mushroom cap a little bigger to hold the filling.
3. Lightly prick the caps from inside with a fork and brush them with a little oil from inside out.
4. Combine chopped parsley / coriander with garlic, celery, salt and pepper and fill the mushroom caps.
5. Prepare a baking dish by brushing it with a little oil. Arrange the mushroom caps in it and sprinkle with olive oil.
6. Bake for 15 to 20 minutes.

Serving: Serve the stuffed roasted mushrooms hot, immediately, as a starter.

Tips: Mushroom stems can be used for any soup or soup stock as mushroom enhances the flavour.

Cooking time: 35 minutes.

13. Chickpeas Patties with Yogurt Dip

Distinctive nutty flavour of these slightly spicy chickpeas patties rolled in rich sesame seeds make this dish stand apart in taste and nutrition.

You Require:

Chickpeas / white channa	2 cups	Garlic paste	2 tsp
Coriander powder	1 tsp	Cumin powder	1 tsp
Black pepper powder	1 tsp	Eggs beaten	2 no
Mint leaves chopped	1 tbsp	Coriander / parsley	1 tbsp
Fresh red / green chilli chopped	2 no	Spring onion chopped	2 no
Black rock salt	1 tsp	Salt	to taste
Sesame seeds to coat		Cooking oil for frying	

Preparation and Cooking:

1. Soak the chickpeas overnight or minimum for 6 hours, drain the soaking water and rinse.

Place chickpeas in a pressure cooker and add fresh water; once the chickpeas start boiling on high flame, place the lid and the pressure knob. Let the pressure build, then lower the heat to medium and cook for 30 minutes.

2. Switch off the fire and wait for 5 to 10 minutes. Open the lid and strain the liquid (save it for soup or some gravy).
3. Place the chickpeas in an electric blender; add the remaining ingredients except the sesame seeds and oil for frying. Blend until the mixture turns into a coarse paste. Remove it from the blender jar.
4. If the chickpeas mixture appears too wet, just chill it for 30 minutes; remove and then form into patties. Roll all the shaped patties in sesame seeds one by one and keep aside.
5. Heat enough oil in a large pan / griddle and shallow fry patties from both the sides turning once. Remove and place on kitchen oil absorb paper for some time.

Serving: Serve it hot as a snack or a side dish with any sauce / chutney or Yogurt dip.

Cooking time: 45 minutes after boiling chickpeas.

14. Onion - Jalapeno Flavoured Cheddar Cheese

Cut any flavoured cheese or cheeses of your choice and arrange on cheese platter or in a tray, and serve along with fresh fruit and wine of your choice.

Serving: Serve as a starter.

15.Risotto Cake

(Budino di riso)

You Require:

Small grain rice	1 cup	Chicken stock	2 and ½ cups
Lemon juice	1 tbsp	Lemon rind	from 1 lemon
Fresh parsley chopped	2 tbsp	Chives dry	½ tsp
Spring onion chopped	1 no	Mozzarella cheese grated	¾ cup
Salt-n-pepper	to taste		

Preparation and Cooking:

1. Preheat the oven to 200 degrees Celsius.
2. Prepare a mould with a loose base, oil it.
3. Boil stock; add spring onion, salt and pepper, add rice and stir, cover the pan and cook on medium heat for 25 to 30 minutes or until the liquid is absorbed.
4. Stir in the lemon juice, rind, herbs and cheese. Mix. Put the mixture in the prepared cake tin and bake for 40 to 45 minutes or until sides appear brown. Turn out.

Serving: Cut the lemon risotto cake in wedges and garnish with parsley and lemon wedges.

Serve it as a main course with a salad. You may serve it as a side dish.

Tips: If you prefer crisp rice cake wedges, before baking put the rice in a bigger mould in a thinner layer.

Cooking time: About 1 hour 20 minutes.

16. Baked Eggs with Tomatoes

(Uova al piatto con pomodori)

An excellent way to eat eggs and tomatoes with crusty bread or dinner rolls, particularly, when fresh tomatoes are in season.

You Require:

Eggs	6 no	Tomatoes	4 no
Tomato puree	¼ cup	Onions chopped	2 medium
Jalapeno chopped	1 no	Garlic paste	1 tsp leveled
Salt-n-pepper	to taste	Cheese grated	2 to 3 tbsp
Fresh basil chopped	2 tbsp	Olive oil	2 tbsp
Or			
Oregano dried	½ tsp		

Preparation and Cooking:

1. Roast tomatoes and remove the skin. Chop them fine and keep aside.
2. Heat oil in a pan and sauté onions; add chopped green chilli and tomatoes along with the garlic; cook till the juices dry and tomato paste looks quite homogeneous. Season it with salt, pepper and oregano or basil.
3. Brush a heat-proof dish with a little oil and spread tomato paste evenly.
4. Make depressions with a spoon and break one egg in each depression. Optionally season mildly with salt and pepper.
5. Sprinkle cheese over eggs and bake in hot oven for almost 20 to 25 minutes or till egg whites are set but yolks are still soft.

   Or

   Cook in a microwave on COMBINATION mode for 10 to 12 minutes.

   Serving: Serve it immediately with bread and vegetable soup as a mini meal.

   Cooking time: 40 to 45 minutes.

17. Calzone

(calzone)

A calzone is made of pizza dough and stuffed with any filling. In fact it is a pizza folded over its filling and then baked. It can be made large or small and can be eaten hot or at room temperature.

You Require:

Whole wheat Pizza dough	½ recipe	Veg / non-veg filling of your choice	2 cups
Cheese grated	½ cup	Baking tray	

Preparation and Cooking:

1. Preheat the oven to moderately hot temperature.
2. Divide pizza dough; filling and cheese into equal portions. Mix cheese and filling.
3. Roll one portion of the dough into a 4 to 5 inch circle; place the filling on half of the circle and cover it with the other half. Finish rolling all the portions in the similar fashion; fill them and fold them.
4. Brush the baking tray with a little oil; place all folded calzones in the tray and bake till golden brown. Cool and serve.

Serving: Serve them at room temperature as a starter with or without a soup.

Cooking time: About 20 minutes.

18. Bruschetta with Tomato

(Bruschetta con pomodoro)

Very simple but excellent starter that can be consumed anytime; its tasty-mild garlic flavoure imparts very satisfying feeling to a diner.

You Require:

Crusty white bread	8 to 12 slices	Tomatoes chopped	4 medium
Garlic peeled	4 cloves	Fresh basil chopped	1 tbsp
Extra virgin olive-oil	4 tbsp	Salt -n-pepper	to taste

Preparation and Cooking:

1. Toast or grill bread from both sides till crisp.
2. Meantime season chopped tomatoes with salt and pepper. Add chopped basil.
3. Now cut the garlic cloves into halves and rub the one side of toasts with it.

Serving: Arrange toasted bread in a platter and sprinkle with olive oil; spoon on the chopped tomatoes with juices and serve immediately as an appetizer or accompaniment.

Cooking time: 20 minutes.

19.Fried Pizza Patties

(Panzerotti)

A popular snack from central and southern Italy often served as hot antipasti, is also made of pizza dough but unlike calzone the patties are fried.

You Require:

Basic pizza dough	Filling of your choice
Oil for frying	

Preparation and Cooking:

1. Make filling with cooked vegetables, shredded chicken, minced mutton or chopped sea food and cool. Flavour it according to your taste with herbs, salt, pepper and spices. The mixture should be dry enough to be stuffed.
2. Divide the dough into lemon sized balls and filling also into equal portions. Roll each portion into a 3 to 4-inch thin disc and stuff it. Place filling on half of the disk, cover it with the other half and seal it properly. Note: For sealing you may apply either water or beaten egg on the edges of the rolled disk. Press the edges properly, so that the patties do not open while frying.
3. Heat cooking oil on full heat; lower the fire and fry the patties, 2 at a time, on medium heat. Remove them on kitchen oil absorbent paper and serve hot

Serving: Serve the patties as a snack.

Cooking time: 35 to 40 minutes.

20. Chicken Breasts Stuffed with Cheese and Ham

(Patte de pollo ala Bolognese)

You Require:

Boneless flattened breasts of chicken 4 pieces large

Lemon juice	2 tbsp	Cheese slices/singles	4 no
Ham slices	4 no	Beaten eggs	2 no
Bread crumbs	1 cup or more	Salt-n-pepper	to taste
Oil	for frying	Lemon juice	2 tbsp

Preparation and Cooking:

1. Flatten the chicken breasts with meat flattener and smear with lemon-juice, salt and pepper for 30 minutes. You may flatten chicken pieces placed between 2 thick plastic sheets one by one.
2. Season beaten eggs with a pinch of salt and pepper each.
3. Take one chicken piece; dry it on kitchen towel and spread it on chopping board. Place 1

piece of cheese on it and then overlap with a ham slice. Fold the sides of chicken breasts over ham and roll it. Dip it in beaten egg and roll in crumbs. Finish rolling all the breasts pieces like this and refrigerate for 30 minutes.

4. Fry one by one on medium hot fire till brown and crisp. Drain on kitchen oil absorbent paper. Slice them before serving.

   Serving: Serve them as starter with any dip or tomato sauce.

   Cooking time: Approximately 2 hours.

21. Prawns on Skewers

(Gamberi skewers)

Very simple but delicious antipasti, a delight to seafood gourmets that can be enjoyed with a variety of wines, anytime.

You Require:

Large prawns	24 no	Bread crumbs	½ cup
Salt-n-pepper	to taste	Lemon juice	3 tbsp
Olive oil	2 tbsp	Cherry tomatoes	24 no
Wooden or metal skewers	6 to 8 no		

Preparation and Cooking:

1. Soak the wooden skewers (if using) in cold water for 1 to 2 hours.
2. Clean prawns and place them in a bowl. Mix together olive oil, lemon juice, salt and pepper in a small bowl and pour over prawns. Stir well. Sprinkle breadcrumbs over the prawns; mix lightly and stand for 30 minutes.
3. Thread alternately 3 to 4 prawns on each skewer and place in one layer under the grill or on a barbeque for 3 to 4 minutes. Turn and cook for another 3 minutes.

   Serving: Serve them on lettuce bed or individually with some salad in serving plates.

   Cooking time: 7 to 8 minutes for each batch.

22.Chili - Tomato Cheese Toasts

These tasty toasts are like open sandwiches which can satiate any time hunger pangs.

You Require:

Crusty white bread	1 no	Mozzarella cheese sliced	
		Chilli-garlic sauce	1 tbsp
Tomato sauce	¼ cup	Oregano	1 tsp

Preparation and Cooking:

1. Cut bread diagonally into thick slices and grill them for 4 to 5 minutes or until lightly toasted.
2. Mix together chilli-garlic and tomato sauce and spread on toasted bread evenly.
3. Place sliced cheese on each piece and grill it again till cheese starts bubbling and is golden brown in colour.
4. Sprinkle oregano lightly and serve.

Serving: Serve it hot or warm as a starter or along with a good soup or a salad as a small meal.

Cooking time: 10 to 15 minutes.

23. Vegetables with Olive Oil Dip

(Pinzimonio)

This colourful starter comes from Rome, where either raw or partially cooked vegetables are served with olive oil dip seasoned with salt, pepper and fresh basil.

You Require:

For olive oil dip:

Olive oil	¼ to ½ cup	Lemon juice	1 tbsp to 3 tbsp
Salt	to taste	Freshly ground pepper	to taste
Basil leaves	4 no chopped		

Fresh vegetables:

You may select any vegetables of your choice

(Asparagus, Broccoli, Cauliflower, Carrots, Cucumber, Tomatoes, Mushrooms, Celery, Radishes and Spring onions etc)

Preparation and Cooking:

1. Steam lightly the vegetables like asparagus stems, cauliflower/broccoli flowerets and carrot sticks. Cool.
2. Mix together olive oil, salt and pepper properly and strain in a small serving bowl; add lemon juice and stir. Garnish with chopped basil.

Serving: Arrange selected vegetables in a platter and serve with the olive oil dip as a starter.

Preparation time: 30 minutes.

24. Tomato Tart

(Torta di pomodori)

Italians use tart for preparing both the sweet and savoury dishes.

You Require:

For the tart:

Flour	1 and ½ cup	Butter / margarine (chilled)	½ cup
Salt	½ tsp	Cold water	5 tbsp

For the filling:

Tomatoes	4 to 5 no	Salamis	12 no
Mozzarella cheese	¾ cup	Salt-n-pepper	to taste
Basil leaves	about 15 in no	Olive oil	2 tbsp
Grated parmesan cheese	3 tbsp		

Preparation and Cooking:

1. Sieve flour and salt together in a bowl. Cut the butter in and mix with pastry blender or your own finger tips until the mixture resembles breadcrumbs / coarse meal.
2. Add 3 tbsp chilled water and start gathering the dough with a fork or with fingertips. Keep sprinkling a little more remaining water and gathering the dough if it is crumbly.
3. Gather the dough into a ball; flatten it in a disc and wrap it in greaseproof paper or a piece of plastic sheet and refrigerate it for 45 minutes.
4. Preheat the oven to 190 degrees Celsius.
5. Cut the salamis into strips and tomatoes into thick slices.
6. Roll the pastry onto a floured platform or between the two plastic sheets to the thickness of ¼ -inch. Fit in a pastry shell or a pie pan trimming the edges evenly. Refrigerate it for 20 minutes.
7. Remove it out; prick the bottom with a fork and bake it blind in the hot oven for about 15 minutes. Remove it. Leave the oven on.
8. Brush the pastry with olive oil and line it with mozzarella cheese. Break half the basil leaves into pieces and sprinkle over cheese.
9. Arrange the tomato slices over the cheese. Place salamis in between and dot with remaining basil.
10. Sprinkle salt, pepper, remaining oil and grated parmesan cheese bake for about 35 to 40 minutes.

Note: If while baking you feel more than required liquid is oozing out, take it out with a small spoon tilting the pastry a bit, so that pastry remains crisp and does not turn soggy.

Serving: Serve the Tomato Tart hot or at room temperature.

Variation: Avoid salamis and fill the tart with any other prepared meat or vegetables. Sprinkle some cheese on top before final baking.

Cooking time: 1 hour.

25. Grilled Fish Kebabs

You Require:

Thick fillets from fresh fish	500 gm	Lemon juice	2 tbsp
Salt-n-pepper	to taste	Onion large	1 no
Basil	a few leaves	Olive oil	for brushing
Peppers large	1 green and red each		
Wooden/metal skewers	6 to 8 no		

Preparation and Cooking:

1. If you are using wooden skewers, soak them in cold water at least for 1 to 2 hours in advance.
2. Cut fish into 2" square pieces and marinate with lemon-juice, salt and pepper. Stand it for 30 minutes.
3. Meantime, cut peppers and onions too in the same size and smear with a little olive oil, salt and pepper.
4. Now, alternately, thread fish pieces and vegetables. You may use 4 to 5 layers only of onion pieces in one go.
5. Place the skewers in single layer under the hot grill or on barbeque and cook for 3 minutes. Turn the side and cook for 3 minutes more. You may grill for 1 minute more (if you prefer more brown) from both the sides.

Serving: Serve each skewer in individual plate with additional wedge of lemon and some sauce.

Cooking time: 6 to 8 minutes for each batch.

26. Batter Fried Prawns

(Gamberelli fritto)

You Require:

Large prawns	500 gm	Flour	½ cup
Oil for frying			
For the Batter:			
All purpose flour	½ cup	Corn flour	¼ cup
Egg white	1 large	Olive oil	1 tbsp
White vinegar	1 tsp	Baking powder	½ tsp

Water	½ cup	Freshly ground pepper	½ tsp
Salt	to taste	Lemon wedges to serve	

Preparation and Cooking:

1. Combine egg white, vinegar and olive oil in a bowl and whisk with an egg beater.
2. Sieve together the dry ingredients and mix in the beaten egg mixture until well blended. Add water a little at a time and whisk again. Cover the bowl and let it stand for 15 minutes.
3. Meantime heat oil in a frying pan. Dredge the fish / prawns in the flour, shaking off excess flour; dip the pieces in the batter and fry in small batches from both the sides till golden in colour.
4. Remove with a slotted spoon and drain on kitchen oil absorbent paper. Finish frying all the pieces in the same fashion. After each lot, heat up oil properly and lower down the heat while putting batter dipped pieces for frying.
5. Sprinkle a little salt over the fish before serving.

Serving: Garnish the dish with lemon wedges and serve it with tomato sauce as a starter, or with garlic sauce as a side dish. In this case heat garlic sauce and toss fried prawns in it.

Variation: You may fry bone-less fish pieces the same way.

Cooking time: About 40 minutes.

27. Italian Meat Balls

(Polpettine)

This tasty preparation is ideal to be eaten as a starter, or in main course to be eaten along with rice /pasta as such, or to be served along with meat sauce over plain spaghetti.

You Require:

Minced mutton	500 gm	Garlic paste	1 tbsp
Fresh chopped basil	2 tbsp	Coriander chopped	2 tbsp
Onion chopped fine	1 medium	Fresh Bread crumbs	½ cup
Egg	1 no large	Cheese grated	3 tbsp
Cooking vinegar	¼ cup	White wine	¼ cup
Water	1 cup	Freshly ground pepper	2 tsp
Mixed Italian herbs	1 tsp	Salt	to taste
Olive oil	3 to 4 tbsp		

Preparation and Cooking:

1. In a bowl combine all the ingredients for the meatballs except water, vinegar, white wine and olive oil; mix them properly and keep aside.
2. Grease your palms lightly with olive oil and form the small balls (about 1-inch in diameter) out of the meat mixture.

3. Heat oil in a heavy bottomed pan with a lid and place the rolled balls in it carefully. Cook the meatballs over high fire, occasionally shaking the pan, so that they are evenly coated with oil and browned from all sides.
4. Add water mixed with vinegar and a pinch of salt in the pan; lower the heat; cover the pan with its lid and cook the balls for 8 to 10 minutes or until cooked through.
5. Add wine to the pan; stir with a light hand and serve. Check the seasonings.

Serving: Garnish the meatballs with chopped coriander / parsley and serve hot.

Tips:

a. You may use beef mince / chicken mince instead of mutton for this preparation.

b. Instead of vinegar, you may use tomato puree.

c. You may use parmesan cheese.

d. To get soft breadcrumbs, grind fresh bread slices.

Cooking time: 30 minutes.

28. Ham Sandwich

You Require:

Sandwich bread	16 slices	Ham	8 slices
Cheese singles	4 slices	Mayonnaise	½ cup
Mustard sauce	¼ cup	Tomato sauce	½ cup
Salad leaves	8 no	Pesto sauce	¼ cup (opt)

Preparation and Cooking:

1. Toast bread slices from one side in a lightly oiled non-stick pan.
2. Mix mayonnaise and mustard sauce together and apply generously on 8 slices; apply tomato sauce on 4 slices and pesto on remaining4 slices.
3. Now assemble into 4 sets. Place 1 piece of ham slice between the 2 slices smeared with mayonnaise; apply sauce on top of second slice too, place a cheese slice; then top with third slice smeared with pesto sauce, apply pesto on other side of slice too, cover it with 2nd leaf of lettuce and ham slice and finally top with a slice having mayonnaise on.
4. Insert 1 tooth-pick temporarily in the centre of the sandwich; press lightly with your palm and remove the sides of bread. Cut the sandwich into desired shape.

Serving: Serve it anytime, on its own or with any beverage, soup or a salad.

Tips: If you have to serve the sandwiches a little later, wrap them in a moist napkin and place in a container, or cover with cling-wrap; and store under refrigeration till used.

Assembling time: 20 to 25 minutes.

29. Melting Mozzarella Snack

This mouth watering dish of mozzarella pieces, coated with flour, dipped in egg and rolled in bread crumbs and finally deep fried, originates from the Neapolitan area where mozzarella cheese is produced in plenty and enjoyed in any form.

You Require:

Mozzarella cheese	250 gm	Eggs beaten	2 to 3 no
Flour	½ to ¾ cup	Bread crumbs	aboul cup
Oil for deep frying		Salt and pepper to season flour	

Preparation and Cooking:

1. Cut mozzarella cheese in any shape you like.
2. Heat oil for frying and lower the heat.
3. Season flour with salt and pepper and spread in a plate.
4. Coat cheese pieces with seasoned flour.
5. Shake off extra flour; dip the pieces in egg and roll in bread crumbs (already spread in a flat dish) and immediately fry on medium high heat to golden brown colour.
6. Drain with a slotted spoon on kitchen paper and serve hot.

Avoid: Keeping breaded cheese pieces for too long.

Serving: Serve the fried pieces immediately.

Cooking time: 30 minutes or so.

❒

Italian Cheese Sauce

Main Course

Chicken Cooked with Red Grapes

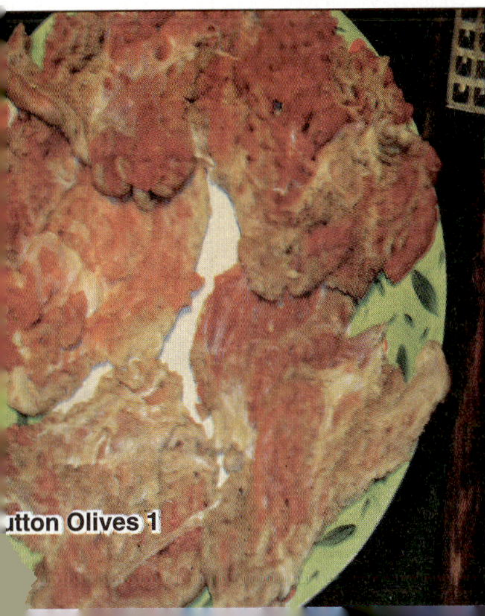

utton Olives 1

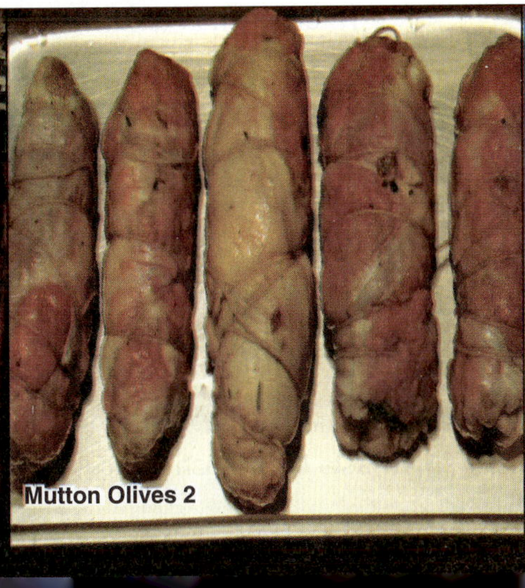

Mutton Olives 2

Mutton Olives Ready to be Served

Lemon Fish

Multicoloured Macroni in Cheese Sauce

Pumpkin Chicken Pie

Saffron Flavoured Chicken Rice

Italian Bread

Ravioli

Stuffed Peppers

Three in One Pasta

Fish Monte Carlo

Roasted Chicken with Lemon and Vegetables

Pasta in Spinach Sauce

Spaghetti in Meat Sauce

Bow Pasta with Green Pesto Sauce

Fried Fish

Chili Garlic Flavoured Broccoli

Chicken Balls in Chili Garlic Sauce

Linguini with Mixed Peppers

Roasted Tomatoes and Garlic

Risotto with Vegetables and Roasted Chicken

Mushroom Stuffed Baked Chicken Rolls

Focaccia

Sweet & Sour Aubergines

Lasagne Cooked with Spinach Sauce

Tagliated Mushroom Pasta with Mushroom Sauce

Canneloni Ripieni Filling

Cannelloni Ripni before Baking

Cannelloni Ripni-ready to be Served

Stuffed Tomatoes with Pasta

Lasagne Cooked with Meat Sauce

Chicken Roasted with Wine and Herbs

Fish Fillets Grilled on Rotisserie

Stuffed Cabbage Rolls

Turkey Rolls

Tomato Rice

Chicken Italiana

Garlic Flavoured Prawn Rice

VARIETY OF PIZZAS

Chicken Pizza Before Baking

Chicken Pizza After Baking

Chicken-Baby Corn- Olives Pizza

Tomatoes, Zucchini and Peppers Pizza

Italian Bread

Mushroom Tomato Pizza Before Being Baked

Mushroom Tomato Pizza

Pizza with Onions, Chicken and Chives

Pizza with Peppers

Spicy Chicken

Tomato Pizza

Jelapeno and Olives Pizza

Main Course

They say that Italian cooks, traditionally, relied on local ingredients cultivated in Italy or gathered from the local wild area (for example, variety of wild mushrooms). It is true to a certain extent. The fact is that the essence of Italian cooking is simplicity. Now-a-days, because of supermarket culture, the variety of flavourful good quality Italian ingredients are made easily available, at least in the bigger cities of the world, so cooking Italian food has become possible for anyone who likes to cook different dishes. Tthe fresh and preserved vegetables play an important part in Italian cuisine; either they are served in their own right as dishes or they are combined with a variety of meats, poultry and sea-food. From antipasti to main course dishes they are an integral part of Italian cooking.

Here, in our recipes, we have tried to give more of vegetarian dishes (as India being mainly a vegetarian country); we have given many recipes for the delight of non-vegetarians too. We have used the veg and non-veg ingredients which are easily available in India. If you reside in any other part of the world, you can use the typical Italian ingredients and cook with the prescribed recipes.

1. Multi-Coloured Macaroni in Cheese Sauce

(Multi coloured fusilli in Cheese sauce)

You Require:

Macaroni boiled	3 cups	Cheese sauce	2 to 2 and ½ cups
Carrots chopped	½ cup	Green peas shelled	½ cup
Green pepper sliced	1 no	Milk	½ cup if required
Cheese grated	¼ cup	Tomato slices	10 to 12
Fresh herbs	¼ cup		
Or			
Oregano	1 tsp		

Preparation and Cooking:

1. Grease a micro-safe dish and keep aside.
2. Boil carrots and peas in a steaming basket for 3 minutes on HIGH.
3. Combine cheese sauce, oregano and fresh herbs together and mix with boiled macaroni and vegetables. If you find the mixture, too thick, add ½ cup milk and check the seasoning.
4. Spread half the pasta mixture in the greased dish; arrange half tomato slices and sliced pepper on top and cover with the remaining pasta mixture.
5. Arrange rest of the tomato and pepper slices on top of the dish and sprinkle grated cheese over them.
6. Bake on COMBINATION mode. Press Combi-1, set time and start. Bake the dish for

15 minutes. If the top is not golden brown, then put the dish under Grill for 3 minutes. Remove and serve.

Or

After step three, just mix the boiled multi-coloured pasta with cheese sauce and serve hot.

Note: This dish can also be baked in hot oven on Convection mode of a microwave /in electric oven or in an oven of a cooking range for 30 to 35 minutes, or till the top is golden brown.

Serving: Serve 'Macaroni baked in Cheese sauce' as a part of any Italian meal.

Since this dish is a complete meal in itself, light soup and a salad are recommended as accompaniment for the day-to-day menu. Party menu can be as elaborate as you wish.

Variation: Cook 200 gm well spiced minced Mutton / Chicken separately and add to the macaroni mixture; and bake in a microwave or in hot oven as recommended in the recipe.

You may or may not omit the boiled vegetables and herbs from the original recipe.

Do not add turmeric powder to the minced meat.

Or

Cook 'Baked Vegetables in Cheese sauce'. Omit macaroni and increase the quantity of steamed vegetables. Add potatoes and cauliflower or broccoli to the existing vegetables and follow the same procedure.

Tips: For this preparation macaroni can be boiled beforehand, vegetables can also be steamed in advance and, of course, cheese sauce, too, can be cooked earlier. Mixing and baking can be done 30 minutes before the meal.

Cooking time: 18 minutes micro cooking.

2.Spaghetti in Meat Sauce

(Spaghetti Bolognese)

You Require:

Boiled spaghetti	3 to4 cups	Cheese grated	¼ cup
Italian tomato sauce	1 recipe		
For Italian Tomato sauce:			
Tomatoes	1000 gm	Olive oil / butter	2 tbsp
Garlic minced	1 tbsp	Mutton minced	300 gm
Mushroom chopped	6 no (opt)	Pepper	1 tsp
Chilli powder	1 tsp	Red pepper flakes	½ tsp
Italian herbs (Oregano)	1 tsp	Water or stock	2 cups
Salt	to taste	Meat balls	16 no (opt)

Preparation and Cooking:

1. Place tomatoes in a blender and puree.
2. Strain through a rice colander so that seeds are separated.
3. In a big micro-safe bowl heat butter for 30 seconds on HIGH and add minced garlic; cook for 1 minute on HIGH and mix minced mutton; cook for 3 minutes on HIGH, stirring once and take it out. Break the lumps if any.
4. In the same bowl combine tomato puree and all other ingredients for Italian sauce except oregano.
5. Cook uncovered on HIGH for 15 minutes, stirring thrice.
6. Add minced mutton and oregano to the tomato sauce and cook it covered for 5 minutes more on HIGH, stirring once in between. Let the sauce stand for 5 minutes before using it.
7. Sprinkle Italian herbs or oregano and chopped parsley or basil. Add meat balls and water.

   Info: This sauce is also known as Italiam meat sauce.

Assembly:

1. In a square or round micro-safe dish add 1 tsp oil and spread it properly.
2. Cover the base with boiled spaghetti; pour hot tomato-meat sauce over it and sprinkle with grated cheese.
3. Cook on COMBINATION mode for 10 minutes. Press Combi-1; set the time and start. The dish can also be baked in Convection mode for 30 minutes.

Serving: Serve hot pasta as a main dish with any Italian meal or with Spinach and Mushroom Soup.

Variation: Cook Italian Tomato Sauce without Minced mutton but add mixed Italian herbs, available in leading stores.

Cooking time: 35 minutes micro cooking.

3. Pasta in Spinach Sauce

You Require:

Spinach cooked	2 cups	Cheese grated	½ cup
Fresh cream	¼ cup	Tomato puree	¼ cup
Onion fried	1 no	Garlic fried	2 tbsp
Green chilli sauce	1 tbsp	Olive oil	2 tbsp
Olives	10 no	Macaroni uncooked	2 and ½ cup
Salt-n-pepper	to taste		

Preparation and Cooking:

1. Slice olives and keep aside.
2. Puree spinach in an electric blender. Remove in a bowl and mix it with cheese, green chilli sauce, fried onion and garlic. Add cream and season it with salt and pepper to your taste.
3. Boil pasta in plenty of salted water in which a few drops of oil is also added till done.
4. Put in a colander to drain and rinse under tap water. Place in a bowl and smear with olive oil, so that pasta is not dry. Cover it to keep warm.

Serving: For serving mix pasta and spinach in the serving dish, garnish with olives and sprinkle some grated cheese. Either just warm it, or for crisp top bake in hot oven for 30 minutes and serve with tomato sauce.

Or

Place boiled pasta in a serving dish; pour spinach sauce in the centre; sprinkle a little more grated cheese over the dish; garnish with olive slices; cover and heat in a microwave for 3 minutes and serve it hot as a main meal dish.

Cooking time: 35 to 40 minutes.

4. Three-in- One Pasta

It is an interesting and innovative way of serving pasta in three different sauces simultaneously. Not only it is pleasing to the eye, but also delicious in taste.

You Require:

Instant noodles	300 gm	Spinach sauce	1 cup
Or			
Angel hair pasta		Italian tomato sauce	1 cup
Cheese sauce	1 cup	Cheese grated	½ cup
Milk	1 cup	Butter	3 tbsp
Onion	1 no	Ginger grated	2 tbsp
Garlic chopped	1 tbsp	Pepper powder	2 tsp
Cream	¼ cup		

Preparation and Cooking:

1. In a large pan boil enough water; add 1 tsp salt and cooking oil; add pasta and cook till crisp soft or until done. Drain and pour cold water over it, so that it is not over-cooked. Now divide it in three portions.
2. In one portion of pasta add grated cheese, milk, salt and pepper powder and 1 tbsp butter. Mix lightly and keep aside.
3. In another bowl add chopped onion fried in 1 tbsp butter; add 1 tsp grated ginger, spinach puree, cream and 1 tsp pepper powder. Mix it with second portion of pasta and check the seasoning.

4. Mix Italian tomato sauce with the third portion of pasta and keep aside.
5. Cut the cheese slices into triangles.
6. Take an ovenproof dish and smear it with a little oil.

Assembling:

1. First place the third portion of pasta with tomato sauce in the dish.
2. Now spread the first portion of pasta with milk and cheese on it gently.
3. And finally place the second portion mixed with spinach on it. Decorate the top with cheese triangles or grated cheese.
4. Bake for 30 minutes in a moderately hot oven.

Or

In a large oven proof rectangular dish place three coloured pasta side by side and garnish with cheese the way you desire.

Note: You may use cut Macaroni instead of spaghetti.

Serving: Serve pasta hot with cream of Tomato Soup and its accompaniments.

Tips: If pasta is boiled earlier; all the sauces are prepared in advance and kept covered under refrigeration, the dish can be assembled just one hour before serving; cooking time will reduce tremendously.

Cooking time: 1 hour.

5. Saffron Flavoured Chicken Rice

(Zafferano Risotto)

A perfect nutritious and delicious dish that is simple to cook, too.

You Require:

Arborio rice	2 cups	Chicken	1 no
Fish chunks	1 cup (opt)	French beans cut	½ cup
Green peas shelled	½ cup	Tomato puree	½ cup
Onion sliced	1 no	Garlic chopped	3 tbsp
Bay leaf	1 no	Saffron	a big pinch
Olive oil	3 tbsp	Chicken stock	4 cups
Pepper powder	2 tsp	Salt	to taste

Preparation and Cooking:

1. Clean and cut chicken into 8 pieces.
2. Soak rice for 30 minutes.
3. Put oil in a large micro-safe bowl; add sliced onion and chopped garlic; stir well and cook, uncovered for 2 minutes on HIGH.

4. Add cut chicken pieces; turn to coat well with oil and cook for 8 minutes on HIGH, covered, turning the chicken pieces once after 5 minutes.
5. Add rice, green peas, beans, fish chunks and saffron; mix well and cook for 2 minutes, uncovered.
6. Add stock, salt, pepper and bay leaf. Cover with a lid and cook for 22 minutes, first 10 minutes on HIGH and next 12 minutes on MEDIUM, stirring once after 6 minutes. Let the dish stand for 5 minutes.

Serving: Serve Chicken Risotto immediately before rice becomes too dry.

Tips: Risotto is an Italian style Saffron flavoured Rice Pulao. In the north of Italy, rice is served as a first course, as creamy Risotto, but you can serve it as a main dish with a salad, soup and Italian bread.

If Arborio rice is not available, use small grained rice for the preparation.

Cooking time: 37 minutes micro cooking.

6. Ravioli

(Ravioli)

Ravioli falls in the category of filled pasta. Small squares of fresh flat pasta are filled with any stuffing of the choice, sealed and then poached before being placed in the sauce. They are either baked or just heated through before serving.

Ravioli- light preparation of pasta enclosing force meat of one kind or other. The fillings for ravioli are numerous; meat, poultry or sweetened filling is used.

You Require:

Flour	100 gm	Olive oil	1 tsp
Egg yolk	1 no	Salt	a pinch
1 cup of veg or non-veg well flavoured stuffing.			
Olive oil	2 tsp	Onion chopped	½ cup
Garlic chopped	2 tbsp	Red chilli powder	1 tsp
Fresh cream	1 cup	Red pepper chopped	¼ cup
Cheese grated	¼ cup + 1 tbsp	Italian herbs	½ tsp

Preparation and Cooking:

1. Mix together flour, oil, egg yolk and salt and make basic noodle dough; keep it covered for 2 hours and use. Divide into 2 portions.
2. Roll basic dough portions into thin discs (chapaties).
3. Place filling at different places on one of the disks and cover with the second one. Cut into squares or roundels and seal with beaten egg or flour mixture (2 tbsp flour mixed with 4 tbsp water).

4. Boil 3 cup water in a micro-safe square dish for 6 minutes and cook raviolis in it for 10 minutes. Remove and keep them warm.
5. Heat oil in a micro-safe bowl for 1 minute on HIGH and add chopped onion and garlic, stir and cook for 3 minutes on HIGH, uncovered, stirring once in between.
6. Add chilli powder, Italian herbs, grated cheese, red pepper and cream. Mix warm raviolis with the cream sauce gently.
7. Transfer the dish into a shallow serving dish; sprinkle with grated cheese and cover with cling film. Prick the film with a fork at one side for steam to release.

Serving: Heat through this Italian dish on REHEAT mode for 2 to 3 minutes and serve it hot with Italian meal.

Ravioli- light preparation of pasta enclosing force meat of one kind or other. The fillings for ravioli are numerous and meat and poultry leftovers may be used for them.

Cooking time: 22 minutes micro cooking.

7. Lasagne Cooked with Meat-Sauce

(Lasagne)

Lasagne is a dish of large strips of flat pasta, meat sauce and cheese. All the ingredients are placed in layers and then baked.

You Require:

Tomato meat sauce	3 cups	Cheese sauce	1 recipe
Parmesan cheese (grated)	½ cup	Lasagne pasta	6 to 8 sheets
Oil	1 tbsp	Large rectangle / square micro-safe / oven-proof dish	

Preparation and Cooking:

1. Boil 4 cups water in a square dish for 6 minutes on HIGH; drop in the lasagne pasta and pour oil; cook on HIGH for 10 minutes; stand for 5 minutes; drain the water and rinse pasta with tap water. Keep them warm. Or cook pasta on gas heat; drain; rinse and keep it warm.
2. Oil a micro-safe dish and spread half of the tomato meat sauce evenly to cover the base.
3. Cover it with boiled lasagne pasta / sheets.
4. Spread cheese sauce over it and sprinkle a little grated cheese, too.
5. Repeat the process one more time and sprinkle grated cheese on top.
6. Cook on micro MEDIUM for 20 minutes or till cheese is melted and the sauce is bubbling hot.

   Or

   Bake in moderately hot oven for 35 to 40 minutes.

   Note: The recipe of Tomato-meat sauce has been given in **'Pasta in Italian meat sauce'**.

Serving: Serve 'Lasagne' hot with Italian meal containing a salad and a filling soup.

Cooking time: 36 minutes micro cooking.

8. Cannelloni Ripieni

(cannelloni)

Cannelloni is a dish of filled and rolled strips of egg pasta baked in cheese sauce. Here, particularly, the dish is made with pancakes and not with ready-made pasta.

You Require:

Cannelloni pasta	12 no	Cheese sauce	1 and ½ recipe
Or			
Pancakes	12 no	Cheese grated	2 tbsp
Stuffing for cannelloni	2 cup		

For Stuffing / Filling:

Onion chopped	1 no	Carrots	2 no
Green peas	½ cup	Pepper	1 no
Parsley chopped	2 tbsp	Egg	1 no
Olive oil / butter	2 tbsp	Garlic chopped and fried	1 tsp
Pepper powder	½ tsp	Salt	to taste

Preparation and Cooking:

1. Heat 3 cups of water in a micro safe bowl on HIGH for 6 minutes and boil cannelloni pasta for 6 minutes; stand it for 3 minutes; drain water and run under the tap. Keep them covered and warm.

   Or

   Roll noodle dough very thin into a large square and cut 3-inch wide and 7-inch long strips as cannelloni pasta and boil in 4 cups of water on HIGH for 6 minutes and drain immediately. Or cook ccnnelloni pasta on gas heat.

   Run under tap and keep them covered and warm.
2. Chop all the vegetables for filling into very fine dices.
3. Steam carrot and green peas for 2 minutes on HIGH and keep covered.
4. Heat oil or butter in a micro safe bowl for 1 minute on HIGH and cook onion and chopped pepper in it for 2 minutes on HIGH.
5. Add steamed vegetables, garlic salt and pepper and mix properly.
6. Beat egg and pour over vegetables; mix and cook for 1 minute on HIGH. Sprinkle parsley and keep aside.
7. Grease one micro safe dish with 1 tsp oil and keep aside.

8. Place 1 cannelloni pasta strip on chopping board; spread 1 tbsp filling and roll it in a cylindrical shape. Finish stuffing and rolling all the strips.
9. Place them in the greased dish and cover with cheese sauce.
10. Sprinkle grated cheese on top and bake in a microwave on COMBINATION - 1 for 15 minutes.

    Or

    Bake in moderately hot oven for 30 minutes.

Serving: Serve 'Cannelloni Ripieni' hot with Italian meal.

Tips: Noodle dough: Make dough with 100 gm flour, 1 egg yolk, 1 tsp cooking oil and a pinch of salt. Stand it for 30 minutes and use.

Cooking time: 33 minutes micro cooking.

9.Polenta with Mushroom Sauce

(Polenta con funghi)

In Italian cookery, especially, 'Polenta' is a breakfast dish, but I am sure, one can enjoy it anytime. The same dish is known as Corn Mush or Sauted Corn Mush in American cookery.

You Require:

Yellow cornmeal (makki-ka-atta)	1 cup		
Water	4 cup	Salt	1 tsp
Italian herbs / oregano	2 tsp	Butter	2 tbsp
Grated cheese	½ cup (opt)	Mushroom sauce to serve with	

Note: the recipe of Mushroom sauce is given in the recipe Chicken Italiana.

Preparation and Cooking:

1. Sift cornmeal and salt together; combine with half the water.
2. Boil remaining water in a micro safe bowl on HIGH for 6 minutes.
3. Gradually add boiled water to cornmeal mixture and stir. Add Italian herbs and 2 tbsp butter in it. Mix properly.
4. Cook for 5 minutes on HIGH, uncovered; take out the bowl and stir the mixture properly.
5. Cover the dish and cook again on HIGH for 5 minutes. Stand it for 5 minutes in the oven.

Serving: Serve it hot with Mushroom sauce. It is delicious to be eaten hot like porridge.

Serving variations:

1. Add grated cheese to the mixture and pour it into a greased baking dish; sprinkle a little more cheese and bake in moderately hot oven until brown.
2. Pour into the greased loaf tin; cover and chill until firm. Cut it into the slices and serve with any of the sauces.

3. Cut the firm polenta into ½ -inch thick slices; coat with cornmeal and shallow fry in hot fat, turning to brown on both sides.

Note: Serve shallow fried pieces with Sauce / Honey / Corn syrup or Maple syrup.

Cooking time: 18 minutes micro cooking.

10.Baked Polenta

You Require:

Cooked polenta	1 recipe	Butter	3 tbsp
Onions	2 medium	Olive oil	2 tbsp
Mozzarella	100 gm		
Or			
Cheddar cheese	100 gm	Nutmeg powder	a pinch
Parmesan cheese grated	¼ cup	Parsley chopped	2 tbsp
		Salt-n-pepper	to taste

Preparation and Cooking:

1. Slice onion thinly and sauté in olive oil till soft, and season with nutmeg powder, salt and freshly crushed pepper.
2. Slice thinly mozzarella or cheddar cheese.
3. Preheat the oven to 190 degrees Celsius.
4. Warm up cooked polenta and stir in 1- tbsp butter in it.

   Spread the mixture on the clean work surface or in a large metal plate in ½ inch thick layer. Let it cool completely and then cut into roundels.
5. Butter an oven proof dish and spread half of the onion mixture in the bottom of the dish. Cover with a layer of polenta roundels and brush lightly with melted butter. Add a layer of the sliced cheese and sprinkle some grated parmesan, too. Repeat the layers starting with a layer of onions and ending with grated parmesan. Dot the top with remaining butter and bake for 30 to 35 minutes or until the cheese melts.
6. Dot the top with remaining butter and bake for 30 minutes or so or until the cheese melts.

   Serving: Serve it hot from the baking dish itself.

   Cooking time: 35 minutes, but cooling of polenta before baking extra.

11. Fish Monte Carlo

In Italian cooking corn is not used much, but in a very few dishes, it is used sparingly in cream style form.

You Require:

White sauce	2 cups	Sweet-corn cream style	1 cup
Corn kernels	½ cup	Bacon rashers	4 to 5 no (opt)
Eggs	2 no	Cheese grated	½ cup
Fresh breadcrumbs	½ cup	Butter	1 tsp
White Fish cooked and flaked	1 and ½ cup		

Preparation and Cooking:

1. Preheat the electric oven for moderate heat.
2. Mix together white sauce, sweet corn cream style and corn kernels.
3. Separate egg yolks and whites. Add yolks to the sauce and mix.
4. Beat egg whites stiff and fold into the sauce.
5. Add grated cheese (saving a little for the top) to the sauce mixture and mix lightly.
6. Grease an ovenproof dish, fill by layering the sauce and fish together, finishing with the sauce.
7. Mix crumbs and butter together with your fingertips and sprinkle over the sauce.
8. Finally sprinkle the dish with remaining cheese and bake in moderately hot oven for 25 to 30 minutes.

Note: You may place the dish in microwave and cook on Combination-1 mode for 15 minutes

Serving: For serving grill the Bacon rashers and place them on top of the dish and serve this delicacy hot with Tomato sauce and crisp toasts.

Info: Monte carlo is in the principality of Monaco on the border of France and Italy.

Cooking time: 15 minutes for preparation and 30 minutes for baking.

12. Italian Bread

(Pitza / Pizza)

"The name Pizza originated from the area around Naples (a way in the South west Italy). It is not certain, however, that the nearby village of Pizza, where the flour for the best pizza dough is grown and grounded, can claim to be its creator. A pizza may first have been made to use up left-over bread dough and tomato sauce, plus whatever sausage, ham or cheese happened to be available" says the **Cordon Bleu book 'Cheese and Savouries'.**

You Require:

Pizza shells	4 no	Red/Green peppers thinly sliced	½ cup
Black Olives halved	8 no	Chicken shredded	1 cup
Mushrooms sliced	1 cup	Jalapeño sliced	¼ cup (opt)
Tomatoes sliced	½ cup	Mozzarella Cheese grated	1and ½ cup

Chili flakes to top the pizza	(opt)	Oregano to top the pizza	(opt)
Pizza Sauce	1 and ½ cup		

Note: You can assemble your pizzas according to your preferred combinations of the meats and vegetables. You may use Pineapple slices, Baby Corn, Corn kernels, any other vegetable of your choice, Sea food, Sausages, Salamis or even Paneer to top your Pizzas.

For Pizza Sauce:

Onion-Tomato paste	1 cup	Tomato puree	1 cup
Chili-Garlic sauce	1 tbsp	Butter	1 tsp
Oregano	2 tsp	Pepper powder	2 tsp
Ajwain	½ tsp	Sugar	1 tsp
Finely chopped capsicum	¼ cup	Chili powder	1 tsp (opt)
Parsley chopped	1 tbsp		
Bay leaf	1 no	Salt	to taste

Preparation and Cooking:

1. Heat butter in a pan and add ajwain (carom seeds) to crackle. Add chopped capsicum and cook for 1 minute on high fire.
2. Now add all the other ingredients for pizza sauce to it except parsley. Mix well and cover with the lid. Cook for 3 minutes and remove the dish. Take out the bay leaf and sprinkle chopped parsley.
3. Preheat the Convection mode of your microwave oven for 15 minutes on 200 degrees Celsius. Or preheat any other electric oven or oven of a cooking range for 20 minutes.

Assembly:

Apply pizza sauce generously on pizza shells. Sprinkle some cheese over them; arrange sliced vegetables or meats artistically and finally top with grated cheese.

Cover the shell nicely from all sides.

Baking: Bake pizzas in hot oven one by one for 10 minutes or till cheese melts. If you own a cooking range 3 to 4 pizzas can be baked at a time.

Serving: Cut the prepared Pizza into wedges and serve hot with Mustard/Tomato Sauce, dry Oregano and Chilli flakes etc, as a starter or as a part of the meal with nutritious soup, fibrous salad and any other Italian dishes.

Tips:

1. Prepared Pizza /stored pizza can be reheated very well in the microwave. Place 1 full pizza (at room temperature) on a paper plate or kitchen paper towel and reheat on HIGH for 1.30 minutes.
2. Working people may use good quality ready-made Pizza sauce to make your own pizzas.

Cooking time: 10 minutes for cooking Pizza sauce and 10 minutes each for baking 1 pizza.

13. Linguini with Mixed Peppers

(Linguini con pepperoni)

Peppers belong to the 'capsicum' family. They were brought to Europe by Columbus who discovered them in Haiti. Peppers are specialty of southern Italy and eaten in many forms. Roasting and peeling the peppers before use, not only enhances the flavour but also makes easier to digest.

You Require:

Penne / any other pasta	2 cups	Red, green and yellow pepper	1 each
Onion chopped fine	1 no	Garlic minced	2 cloves
Olive oil	4 tbsp	Parsley chopped	3 tbsp
Salt and fresh ground pepperto taste			

Preparation and Cooking:

1. Char the peppers over direct fire or under a grill till black blisters appear on all sides. Place in a plastic bag and keep aside for 5 to 10 minutes.
2. Place water to boil the pasta.
3. Meantime, peel the peppers; cut them into halves; remove the seeds and stems and slice them into thin stripes.
4. Add 1 tbsp salt and 1 tbsp oil to the boiling water and lower in the pasta. Cook it till crunchy soft; drain water and place it in a bowl and smear with a little oil. Cover and keep it warm.
5. Heat oil in a large pan and sauté onion in it till transparent, add garlic and cook for another minute or two.
6. Mix pepper, salt and onion and stir till peppers are well coated with oil. Sprinkle parsley over it and stir.
7. Pour it over the boiled pasta and mix gently with a fork.
8. Cover and reheat in a microwave for 3 minutes on HIGH. Or mix boiled pasta with vegetables in the pan (step no 6) and constantly stir for 3 minutes on medium heat.

   Serving: Serve it piping hot with tomato sauce and grated Parmesan cheese separately.

   Cooking time: 40 minutes.

14. Mutton Olives

A dish of boneless mutton stuffed with forced meat, baked in the shape of olives and placed in brown gravy, is a delicacy; as Italians enjoy cooking many dishes in this fashion with a variety of meats and a variety of fillings.

You Require:

Boneless mutton	1000 gm	Wine Vinegar	½ cup

Salt	1 and ½ tsp	Pepper powder	1 tsp
Ginger and garlic paste	1 tbsp each	Olive oil	¼ cup
A meat flattener			
Forced meat / Stuffing:			
Onion chopped	¼ cup	Bread slices	3 no
Egg	1 no	Butter	1 tbsp
Parsley chopped	1 tbsp	Salt-n-pepper	to taste
For Brown Gravy:			
Tomatoes chopped	3 no large	Carrot chopped	1 large
Onion sliced	1 no	Cardamom brown	3 no
Cloves	6 no	Cinnamon	1-inch piece
Peppercorns	12 no	Butter	1 tbsp
Flour	2 tbsp	Bay leaves	2 no
Mutton stock	4 cup	Seasonings	to taste

Preparation and Cooking:

1. Buy 1000 gm mutton and get it boneless. Get boneless meat cut into 50 to 60 gm pieces. Use the bones for making stock to be used in gravy/sauce.
2. Marinate mutton pieces with vinegar, salt and pepper and stand it for 6 hours or overnight under refrigeration, so that meat gets tender.
3. Take the meat out of the fridge and strain the liquid. Save the liquid. Place 1 piece meat on the chopping board or on the clean working surface and flatten it with meat flattener, change the side of the piece and spread a little ginger and garlic pastes on it and beat again till the mutton piece looks like a sheet. If, somehow, the mutton pieces are small, beat 2 to 3 pieces together to make it bigger. Finish flattening all the pieces the same way.
4. Heat butter for forced meat and sauté chopped onion in it. Place the bread slices in a blender to make soft bread crumbs; add them to the onions and stir well; break the egg into it and stir again. Remove from fire and season it with salt, pepper and parsley.
5. Preheat your oven for moderate heat.
6. Place 1 flattened mutton piece on the chopping board; spread a little stuffing on it; roll it in a cylindrical shape like an olive and tie it loosely with a thread. Finish stuffing, rolling and tying rest of the pieces the same way.
7. Dip each roll in the olive oil and place it in a baking tray. Cover it with aluminum foil and place it in the hot oven. Cook the mutton olives covered for 20 minutes and then cook further for 20 minutes uncovered.
8. Meantime prepare brown gravy. Heat butter in a pan and brown sliced onion in it on high fire till very dark in colour (almost on the verge of burning); add other vegetables and spices for the gravy and stir; sprinkle flour on the vegetables and cook on high fire, so that

flour starts sticking to the bottom of the pan. Pour in 3 cups of stock and bring it to the boiling point; lower the heat and simmer for 30 to 40 minutes. Add the saved liquid from the mutton marinade too, and cook till the vegetables are tender. Remove from fire and cool.

Or

After adding stock to the vegetables, cook them covered in a microwave for 10 minutes on HIGH, give standing time of 10 minutes and cool.

9. Pass them though a liquidizer and strain through a sieve. While straining add rest of the stock

10. Remove the mutton olives from the oven, cool slightly and cut off the thread of each olive with a pair of small scissors.

Transfer them to an ovenproof dish; pour brown gravy over olives; sprinkle 1 tsp oregano over it and cook in the oven once again for 20 minutes, covered. If any liquid is left in the baking tray in which olives were baked, add that too, to the gravy. Or

Cover the dish of olives and gravy with a lid or cling film and cook in the microwave for 8 minutes on micro HIGH. Stand it for 5 minutes and serve.

Serving: Serve 'Mutton Olives' with crusty bread with Italian meal.

Tips: This dish is a delicacy for the mutton lovers, so cook it with great care. Avoid cooking it just by the way, but plan its cooking properly.

Cooking time: 1 hour 30 minutes.

15. Red Chili Pasta

Red chili pasta is rarely available in Indian markets; once in a while you come across it in certain stores. One must try it whenever available as it is just delicious.

You Require:

Pasta with red chili	250 gm	Skinned – chopped tomatoes	1 cup
Extra virgin olive oil	2 tbsp	Chopped olives	¼ cup
Garlic minced	1 tbsp	Red pepper chopped	1 small
Oregano	½ tsp	Grated cheese of your choice	¼ cup
Chopped parsley	1 tbsp	Salt	to taste

Preparation and Cooking:

1. Heat oil in a big pan and sauté garlic, parsley, oregano and red peppers; add tomatoes and cook for 5 minutes, covered
2. Boil pasta in plenty of hot boiling water with a little salt and 2 tsp oil until 'al dente' / done. Drain.
3. Add boiled pasta to the sauce, stir and cook for 3 minutes.

4. Add cheese and chopped olives.

Serving: Serve it hot in any meal.

Cooking time: 25 to 30 minutes.

16.Chicken with Basil Cream Sauce

(Pollo in basillico creama)

You Require:

Chicken breasts	4 no	Flour	3 tbsp
Olive oil	1 tbsp	Butter	1 tbsp
Salt and freshly ground pepper			
For Basil cream sauce:			
Butter	1 tbsp	Crushed garlic	2 cloves
Chicken stock	1 cup	Cream	½ cup
Lemon juice	¼ cup	Basil finely chopped	2 tbsp
Fresh ground pepper	¼ tsp	Salt	to taste

Preparation and Cooking:

1. Sieve together flour, salt and pepper in a plate and coat chicken pieces with the mixture evenly, shaking off the excess.
2. Heat the butter and oil in a heavy bottomed pan, add the chicken and cook over the medium heat for 5 to 6 minutes each side. Remove from the pan; cover it and keep it warm.
3. Make basil sauce. Clean the pan with a kitchen towel and heat butter for the sauce. Add the crushed garlic and sauté for 2 minutes; add the chicken stock, cream and lemon juice; cook and reduce the sauce to half. Add basil just before serving. Season it with salt and pepper.

Serving: You may serve the dish in individual plates. Place 1 warm chicken breast in each plate and pour the sauce over it. Serve it with any bread and a salad / soup as a main course dish.

Cooking time: Preparation time 5 minutes and cooking time 15 to 20 minutes.

17. Fish Fillets Grilled on Rotisserie

You Require:

Ravas / Surmai thick fish fillets (or any other fish of your choice)	750 gm	Extra virgin olive oil	2 tbsp
Lemons	3 no	Lemon rind	1 tsp
Garlic paste	2 tsp	Dry Oregano	1 tsp
Coarsely ground pepper	½ tsp	Peppers of any colour	2 no

Preparation and Cooking:

1. Make a marinade: Grate 2 lemons in a small bowl and collect lemon rind. Squeeze lemons into the bowl and mix with olive oil, oregano, garlic paste, a little salt and pepper. Cut the remaining lemon in to 2 halves.
2. Cut fish in thick pieces and marinate it with prepared marinade; and stand it for 45 minutes to 1 hour.
3. Cut pepper also in 2-inch squares and marinate with a little salt, pepper and a few drops of oil.
4. Heat electric oven for 10 minutes; or the convection mode of your microwave to 220 degrees Celsius for 5 minutes.
5. Take out the fish pieces and don't discard the marinade. Thread fish pieces on the rotisserie, starting with a lemon half and then following fish, alternating with a piece of pepper in between, end with the second half of a lemon. Brush the fish with the remaining marinade. Set the rotisserie in the hot oven and grill each lot for 30 to 35 minutes.

Note: If you do not have rotisserie in your oven, cook the fish under a grill placing on oven's high stand; turning the side after 15 minutes. You can also grill the fish in any cooking range. You might have to cook fish in 2 batches.

Remove the rotisserie out of the oven with its stand, unlock and slide the fish with a fork.

Serving: Serve the grilled fish with additional lemon juice, pepper or flavoured salt with Oregano in it, as a starter.

Cooking time: 45 minutes.

18. Bow Pasta with Green Pesto Sauce

(Farfalle green pesto)

You Require:

Bow pasta	2 cups	Green pesto	1 cup
Olive oil	2 tbsp	Green peas shelled	2 cups
Fresh ground pepper	1tsp heaped	Salt	to taste

Preparation and Cooking:

1. Cook bow pasta in boiling salted water with 2 tbsp cooking oil in it till done. Drain and rinse under the tap. Place in a lightly oiled serving bowl, cover and keep it warm.
2. Steam green peas in the steaming basket for 4 minutes with ¼ cup water underneath.
3. Heat oil in a large pan; add green peas, pesto sauce, salt and pepper. Stir nicely and add boiled pasta. Stir with a light hand to coat well with sauce. Reheat before serving.

Serving: Serve it as a main dish along with a nice soup.

Cooking time: 30 to 35 minutes.

19. Chicken Italiana

(Pollo alla Rome)

This preparation of chicken tastes excellent when eaten with mushroom sauce and steamed vegetable such as baby potatoes tossed in a little butter and herbs and or steamed and lightly tossed vegetables. Served with a light soup, it makes complete meal.

You Require:

Chicken legs	8	no	Wine vinegar	¼	cup
Garlic paste	1	tsp	Salt	1	tsp
Pepper powder	1	tsp	Red chili powder	½	tsp
Egg	1	no	Flour	¼	cup
Breadcrumbs	1	cup	Cooking oil for shallow frying		
For Mushroom sauce:					
Mushrooms chopped fine	100	gm	Onion chopped	1	no
Tomato chopped	1	large	Garlic chopped fine	6	cloves
Green pepper chopped	1	small	Red wine	¼	cup
Italian seasonings	1	tsp	Freshly crushed pepper	1	tsp
Tomato-puree	2	tbsp	Salt	to	taste
Olive oil	2 to 3	tbsp	Chicken stock / water	1	cup
Fresh mint chopped	2	tbsp			
Steamed and tossed vegetables to serve with					

Preparation and Cooking:

1. Wash and clean chicken legs. Mark gashes on the chicken pieces with a sharp knife; marinate with wine vinegar, garlic, salt, pepper and chili powder and stand for 6 hours or keep overnight under refrigeration.
2. Mix together flour and bread crumbs in a plate and season it lightly with salt and pepper.
3. Beat egg.
4. Take out the chicken and strain through a colander, saving the liquid. Keep it aside for 30 minutes.
5. Meantime, make mushroom sauce. Heat olive oil in a pan; sauté onion and garlic in it; add mushrooms, pepper and tomato; stir for 3 minutes and then add stock or water. Add the saved liquid from the chicken. Bring the mixture to the boiling point and then lower the heat; simmer it for 15 minutes; add tomato puree, red wine, herbs and pepper powder; check the salt and simmer for 5 minutes more. Cover it. Add chopped mint before serving.
6. Flatten the chicken pieces lightly with a meat flattener; dip them in beaten egg one by one and roll in flour mixture nicely.

7. Heat cooking oil in a medium sized pan for shallow frying; fry chicken pieces on medium heat, 2 at a time, from both sides and drain on kitchen oil absorbent paper.

Serving: Arrange fried chicken in a platter; surround with tossed vegetables and garnish with mint. Serve the Mushroom sauce as an accompaniment to the chicken.

Cooking time: 50 to 60 minutes.

20. Fried Fish

(Fritto-Fisto)

You Require:

Fish fillets	8 no	Lemon juice	3 tbsp
Salt	1 tsp	Flour	1 cup
Cheese powder	½ cup	White pepper powder	1 and ½ tsp
Italian seasonings	1 tsp	Salt	to taste
Eggs	2 to 3 no	Bread crumbs	1 cup or more
Oil for frying			

Preparation and Cooking:

1. Mix lemon juice and 1 tsp salt together and marinate fish fillets with it for 30 minutes. You may marinate fish with Teriyaki sauce, if you desire.
2. Drain fish.
3. Combine flour, cheese, salt, pepper powder and Italian seasonings; mix well and spread in a plate.
4. Beat eggs.
5. Spread bread-crumbs too in a plate.
6. Dredge each fish fillet with seasoned flour; dip in egg and then roll it in bread-crumbs. Finish dredging, dipping and rolling all the fillets and keep under refrigeration for 30 minutes.
7. Heat oil in a frying pan and fry one fillet at a time from both the sides until golden brown. Fry the remaining pieces in the same fashion and place on kitchen paper for extra oil absorption.

Serving: Serve the fried fish with a salad and a sauce. Or serve it with some rice and vegetables as a complete meal.

Cooking time: 1 hour 15 minutes.

21. Stuffed Peppers

(Peperoni ripieni)

Italians stuff their peppers with various fillings made of vegetables, rice, pasta and minced meats and then bake. They even utilize the leftover rice, pasta or vegetables to stuff them and turn into a tasty colourful dish.

You Require:

Peppers (any colour)	6 no	medium	Rice	1	cup
Spring onions chopped (with greens)	4 no				
Tomatoes chopped	4 no	medium	Garlic chopped fine	4	cloves
Parsley / coriander chopped	4	tbsp	Oregano dried	1	tsp
G. Chili deseeded & chopped	1 big	(opt)	Parmesan grated	about 5	tbsp
Olive oil	3 to 4	tbsp	Salt	to	taste
Freshly ground peppercorns	2	tsp	Mozzarella cheese cubed fine	½	cup

Preparation and Cooking:

1. Boil rice till 2/3rd cooked; drain well and keep them warm.
2. Cut peppers into halves lengthwise or remove the tops; blanch in a large pan of boiling hot water for 3 minutes and immediately drain; and place them upside down on a rack to drain well.
3. Preheat the oven to 200 degrees Celsius. Prepare a baking tray by oiling it with a brush lightly.
4. Meantime, heat oil in a large pan and sauté onions, add greens and garlic, stir fry for 1 minute; add tomatoes and chili and cook till the mixture is almost dry; sprinkle oregano; mix and remove from fire.
5. Add boiled rice and cubed mozzarella cheese; mix nicely; sprinkle parsley, salt and pepper; mix once again and check the seasonings.
6. Wipe peppers dry with a kitchen napkin carefully; stuff peppers with the rice filling and top them with grated parmesan cheese.
7. Arrange them in a baking tray and bake for 20 to 25 minutes.

Serving: Serve the peppers hot or at room temperature with tomato sauce.

Tips: Blanching the peppers first helps to make them tender and easy to digest. Instead of blanching, you may cook empty pepper shells for 2 minutes on HIGH in a microwave. Cool and stuff.

Cooking time: 50 to 60 minutes.

22. Risotto with Vegetables and Roasted Chicken

(Risotto con vegetable e pollo)

Although, traditionally, the rice is served as a starter in Italy but it also makes an excellent supper dish with hot crusty bread. You may serve additional grated cheese along. Cheese is an important ingredient of the dish.

You Requre:

Arborio risotto rice	1 cup	Shallots	½ cup
Olive oil	3 tbsp	Fried chicken diced	2 cups
Green Peas	½ cup	Carrot cubed	½ cup
Green pepper diced	1 medium	Grated Parmesan cheese	½ cup or less
Tomato puree	2 tbsp	Salt	to taste
Pepper freshly crushed	2 tsp leveled	Chicken Stock hot	3 and ½ cup
Dry white wine	½ cup		

Note: Leftover roasted chicken breasts can also be diced for this preparation.

Preparation and Cooking:

1. Wash and strain the rice.
2. Heat oil in a pan; add shallots and sauté.
3. Add rice and fry for one or two minutes; add wine, ½ cup stock and seasonings. Stir for a while and add remaining stock. Add vegetables
4. and stir.
5. Bring the mixture to the boiling point; lower the heat; cover the rice and cook for 20 minutes. At this point add tomato puree and cubed chicken; stir gently; cover and cook for 10 minutes more on low heat. Add half the grated cheese and mixed gently with a fork.

   Serving: Serve the rice hot garnished with remaining cheese.

   Cooking time: 35 to 40 minutes.

23.Lemon Fish

(Sogliole al limone)

This classic recipe of the sole fish is a delicacy with the prominent taste of lemon.

You Require:

Fillets of Sole fish	4 no	Plain flour	¼ cup
Salt	1 tsp leveled	Freshly ground pepper	1 tsp leveled
Lemon juice	5 tbsp	Olive oil	¼ cup
Bottled green/red peppercorn	1 tbsp	Butter	1 tbsp
Red salsa to serve with			

Preparation and Cooking:

1. Combine 1 tbsp lemon juice and a large pinch of salt and smear the fish fillets with it. Keep aside for 30 minutes.
2. Season flour with salt and pepper and sieve once, so that it is well mixed. Coat the fish fillets with it evenly from both sides.
3. Heat oil in a thick bottomed frying pan; place two fillets at a time and fry on medium high fire for 2 to 3 minutes from each side. Lift the fillets and place them on a serving plate. Fry the other two fillets in the same manner.
4. Lower the heat and add butter and the lemon juice to the fried oil. Increase the heat and stir the oil mixture until sizzling and golden in colour. Remove the pan from fire and add bottled pepper corns.
5. Pour the lemon mixture over the fried fillets. Sprinkle additional salt and pepper if required and serve.

Serving: Garnish the fish with lemon wedges and serve at-once with or without Tomatoes-Chili salsa.

Tips: For Tomatoes-Chili salsa Combine together finely chopped 2 medium tomatoes, 1 clove garlic, 1 fresh red chili deseeded, 1 tbsp parsley, 2 tbsp extra virgin olive oil, 1 tbsp lemon juice and ½ tsp sugar. Season the mixture with salt and pepper.

Cooking time: 30 minutes.

24. Roasted Tomatoes and Garlic

(Pomodori al forno)

An easy to cook, simple and a tasty dish that becomes an integral part of a roasted meat, soup and crusty bread meal.

You Require:

Plum tomatoes (ripe)	12 no		
Or			
Any other medium sized tomatoes		Garlic cloves	16 to 20 no
Extra virgin olive oil	5 tbsp	Freshly crushed peppercorns	12 to 14 no
Oregano dry	1 tsp		
Fresh oregano or celery leaves for garnishing			

Preparation and Cooking:

1. Preheat the oven to 230 degrees Celsius.
2. Halve the tomatoes lengthwise carefully (keeping the stem intact if possible).
3. Place the tomatoes in an ovenproof shallow dish and place unpeeled garlic cloves in between.

4. Brush the tomatoes with olive oil and sprinkle pepper all over the top.
5. Bake tomatoes in hot oven for 40 to 45 minutes until the tomatoes are sizzling and charred around the edges.
6. Season the dish with salt and dry oregano. You may use extra pepper for the taste.

Serving: Garnish the tomatoes and serve as a part of a main meal.

Cooking time: 50 minutes.

25. Focaccia

(Focaccia)

Focaccia is a form of flat bread which is oiled before baking. It is made in a large baking tray and cut into squares before using it.

You Require:

Basic Pizza dough risen once1 recipe		
Olive oil	3 tbsp	Coarse sea salt

Preparation and Cooking:

1. When the basic pizza dough has risen once, punch it down and knead for 3 to 4 minutes.
2. Brush a flat large tray with 1 tbsp olive oil; place the dough in the pan and press it with your fingers into an even layer of 1 inch thick flat bread. Cover the dough with a cloth and leave it to rise in a warm place for 30 minutes.
3. Preheat the oven for 200 degrees Celsius.
4. Before baking make rows of light dents on the dough with your finger tips; brush with the remaining oil and sprinkle lightly with coarse salt.
5. Bake for 30 minutes or till turn golden. Remove and cut into square pieces or wedges if the bread is baked round.

Serving: Serve it as an accompaniment to a meal or a soup / stew; or serve it alone warm or at room temperature.

Variation: Sprinkle the bread with herbs like rosemary before baking or top it with sauted onions or olives.

Baking time: 30 to 40 minutes.

26. Chicken Cooked with Red Grapes

(Pollo al uva)

This dish perfectly appeals to all the five senses. It is attractive to the eye and flavourful to the tongue. Its rich colour (due to red wine) and sweet-n-spicy flavour (due to red pesto and grapes) makes this dish unique. It's light on stomach, too

You Require:

Chicken breasts	2, cut into 4 pieces	Red pesto	2 tbsp
Red onion sliced	1 medium	Olive oil	3 tbsp
Water	1 and ½ cups	Red grapes halved	1and ½ cups
Salt and pepper	to taste	Red wine	¾ cup
Basil for garnishing			

Preparation and Cooking:

1. Heat 2 tbsp oil in a large shallow pan and saute chicken breasts in it, on medium fire, for about 6 minutes turning the pieces once in between. Remove them with a slotted spoon and drain.
2. Add remaining oil in the pan; add sliced onions and cook till transparent. Add red pesto sauce and cook for 1 minute or so. Mix water and red wine in it and bring the mixture to the boiling point; add chicken pieces, salt and pepper; cover the pan; reduce the heat and simmer for about 20 minutes until the chicken is tender. Stir occasionally.
3. Add grapes to the pan and cook over low fire until heated through. Check the seasonings. Garnish it with basil.

Serving: Serve the chicken hot along with crusty bread and any crisp leafy salad.

Tips: When red grapes are not in season, you may cook the dish with green grapes, green pesto and white wine. Certainly, presentation will look different.

Cooking time: 30 to 35 minutes.:

27. Prawns Cooked in Their Shells

(Gamberi fritti in padella)

This simple dish of prawns cooked in their shells is enjoyed the best when eaten with hands and its juices are mopped up with chunky bread.

You Require:

Fresh large prawns (in their shells)	24 no.	Parsley chopped	2 tbsp
Olive oil	3 tbsp	Garlic chopped fine	2 tbsp
Passata sauce	2 tbsp	Dry white wine	½ cup
Or			
Chili-garlic sauce	2 tbsp	Salt-n-pepper	to taste
White vinegar	½ cup	Crusty bread to serve with	

Preparation and Cooking:

1. Heat oil in a large pan; add prawns and stir over medium fire until they turn pink in colour.
2. Add garlic to the pan and stir again. Mix wine or vinegar and keep stirring constantly to get cooked evenly. By now prawns also absorb the flavor of the garlic.
3. Add passata sauce, salt and pepper and stir till well coated. Shift to serving plate and serve hot.

Serving: Sprinkle parsley over prawns and serve with bread.

Tips: Since prawns are to be enjoyed with hands and they are juicy too, keep mopping the juices with bread and enjoy. Keep the hand tissues handy.

Cooking time: 20 minutes.

28. Turkey Rolls

This simple but elegant turkey dish is not only tasty but also very impressive to look at. It can be served as one of the main course dishes.

You Require:

Slices of turkey loaf	6 to 8 no		
For filling:			
Ham chopped fine	1 cup	Spring onions sliced	2 no
Green chili chopped	1 no	Olive oil	1 tbsp
Egg beaten	1 no	Salt-n-pepper	to taste
For sauce:			
Tomatoes	2 sliced	Onion chopped	1 no
Red pepper chopped	½ no	Italian seasonings	½ tsp
Olive oil	2 tbsp	Salt-n-pepper	to taste
Parsley chopped	1 tbsp		

Preparation and Cooking:

1. Heat oil and sauté spring onions; add green chilies and stir; now add chopped ham, beaten egg ad seasonings; finally stir well on medium heat to coat well and remove from fire.
2. Make sauce. Heat oil and sauté chopped onions in it, add tomatoes and red pepper, cook for a few seconds; add seasonings and cook till the tomatoes are mushy. Cool.
3. Pass the mixture through an electric blender; strain the sauce through a sieve and adjust salt and pepper. Sprinkle a few drops of water to adjust the consistency of the sauce.
4. Assemble. Place each slice of turkey on the working board; spread 1 tbsp stuffing over it and roll it tightly. Finish filling and rolling all the slices and then arrange them in a shallow oven-proof dish.

5. Pour the smooth sauce over the rolls. Loosely cover the dish with a piece of foil and heat up in the hot oven for 10 minutes.

   Or

   Cover the dish with cling wrap and heat it for 3 minutes on REHEAT mode (in a microwave).

Serving: Garnish the turkey rolls with chopped parsley and serve it hot with Garlic toast or Cheese toasts and a Veg. soup.

Variation: Use chicken loaf slices instead of turkey and chopped mushrooms instead of ham, and follow rest of the procedure.

Cooking time: 45 minutes.

29. Pumpkin Chicken Pie

(Tortino di pumpkin e pollo)

This savoury pie, vegetarian or non-vegetarian preparation is almost a meal in itself. Ideally served in the colder weather, it is more enjoyable.

You Require:

Pumpkin peeled	700 gm	Potatoes	400 gm
Green peas (shelled & boiled)	1 cup	Onion chopped	1 no medium
Garlic chopped	2 tbsp	Butter	3 tbsp
Boiled chicken shredded	2 cups	Ricotta cheese	½ cup
Parmesan cheese	½ cup grated	Olive oil	3 tbsp
Pepper crushed	1 tbsp leveled	Italian herbs	1 tbsp leveled
Paprika	2 tsp	Cinnamon powder	1 tsp
Clove powder	1 tsp	Eggs separated	4 no
Salt	to taste	Nutmeg	a pinch
Parsley fresh chopped	for garnishing		

Preparation and Cooking:

1. Preheat an oven to 200 degrees Celsius.
2. Cut pumpkin and potatoes in cubes.
3. Heat olive oil in a pan, add chopped onion and garlic and fry for a while on high fire. Add pumpkin and potato cubes; stir well; add ½ cup water and cover the pan and cook on medium fire till both the vegetables are soft and tender. Stir once in between to avoid sticking to the bottom. Cool slightly.

   Or cook the vegetables covered in a microwave oven for 10 minutes on HIGH, after adding to onion and garlic.
4. Place the vegetables in a large working bowl or in a trove and mash well with butter when

still warm.

5. Mash ricotta cheese with a fork and add to mashed vegetables. Stir in the grated parmesan, pepper, herbs, nutmeg, salt and paprika. Mix well till almost creamy.
6. Add egg yolks, chicken and green peas. Mix once again and check the salt.
7. Whisk egg whites stiff and fold with a light hand into the mixture.
8. Transfer the mixture into the greased baking dish and bake in the hot oven for 45 minutes or so, or till the crust is golden and firm.

Serving: Garnish the dish with parsley and serve it hot with Chili-garlic sauce, crisp Melba toast and a clear Soup.

Variation: Cook it vegetarian without shredded chicken.

Or use mutton mince instead of chicken and follow the process.

Cooking time: 1 hour 15 minutes.

30. Tomato Rice

(Risotto con pomodori)

You Require:

Small brown rice	1 cup	Olive oil	2 tbsp
Spring onions with greens	4 no	Garlic chopped	1 tbsp
Fresh mint chopped	2 tbsp	Tomato sauce	¼ cup
Tomato puree	½ cup	Salt	to taste
Freshly crushed Pepper	½ tsp	Vegetable stock	3 cups
Grated Parmesan cheese	¼ cup		
Or			
Cheese according to taste			

Preparation and Cooking:

1. Wash rice and soak for 15 minutes. Drain and keep in a strainer.
2. Clean and chop spring onions and greens.
3. Heat oil in a deep pan and sauté onions and garlic in it. Add rice and veg stock. Let the mixture boil; add salt and pepper and cook on low fire for 15 minutes, covered with a lid.
4. Open the pan and add tomato sauce, tomato puree and chopped mint. Stir; cover the pan and cook again for 15 minutes. Switch off the fire / heat.
5. Open the lid and check the seasonings. Sprinkle grated cheese and mix lightly. Cover and stand the rice for 5 minutes.

Note: You may increase the quantity of rice as well as the other ingredients proportionately.

Serving: Serve the rice hot garnished with mint leaves or chopped greens of spring onions.

Variation: You may use Chicken stock instead of veg. stock and add ½ cup cleaned shrimps or small pieces of roasted chicken at stage 4 and follow the procedure.

Cooking time: 40 to 45 minutes.

31. Roasted Chicken with Lemon and Vegetables

This simple and delicious roasted dish is just ideal for a light meal in any season.

You Require:

Chicken breasts	cut into 6	pieces	Potatoes cut into 4 pieces each	3	no
Onions cut into large pieces	2	no	Mushrooms	12	no
Peppers cut into large chunks	2 to 3	no	Beans cut into halves	10 to	12 no
Lemons	2	no	Garlic cloves	6 to 8	no
Oregano dry	1	tsp	Cinnamon powder	1	tsp
Chicken stock	½	cup	Olive oil	2 to 3	tbsp
Salt and pepper	to	taste			

Preparation and Cooking:

1. Preheat the oven to 200 degrees Celsius.
2. Squeeze lemon juice, mix it with salt, pepper and 1 tbsp oil; rub it thoroughly on chicken pieces and keep aside. Stand it for 1 hour.
3. Prepare the vegetables and toss them together with garlic, oregano, cinnamon, remaining oil and seasonings.
4. Now arrange chicken pieces and vegetables in a heavy oven-proof dish and bake for 20 minutes.
5. Remove the dish and baste the chicken with its juices; add stock and place the dish again in the hot oven. Bake for 25 to 30 minute more or till the chicken is cooked. In between baste the chicken once more with the pan juices. juices and turn the side. Once cooked remove the dish form oven and cover it with foil for 5 to 10 minutes.

Serving: Serve the dish hot along with any light soup and bread.

Cooking time: 45 to 50 minutes.

32. Mushroom Stuffed Baked Chicken Rolls

This is an innovative dish which has been prepared in Italian style as they love stuffing their meats with a number of ingredients.

You Require:

For marinade:

Chicken breasts	2	no	Lemon juice	4	tbsp
Garlic paste	1	tbsp	Green chilli paste	1	tsp
Salt	1	tsp			

Marinade for chicken:

Make 4 to 6 fillets out of chicken. Combine garlic, chilli paste, salt and lemon juice in a bowl and rub on the chicken pieces generously and keep aside for 4 hours. You may keep under refrigeration overnight. Take them out and flatten each piece one by one with the meat flattener or a rolling pin. Cover and keep aside.

Ingredients for stuffing:

Mushrooms chopped fine	200 gm	Onion chopped fine	1 medium
Parsley chopped fine	2 tbsp	Chilli-garlic sauce	1 tbsp
Fresh breadcrumbs	from 2 slices	Olive oil	2 tbsp
Salt-n-pepper powder	optional	Foil cut into 4 to 6 pieces	(9"x 12")
Mushroom dip to serve with			

Preparation and Cooking:

1. Heat oven to 180 degrees Celsius.
2. Keep a baking tray ready.
3. Heat oil and sauté onions, add mushrooms and cook till the mixture is almost dry. Add remaining ingredients and mix properly over the fire. Filling should be dry. Divide it into equal portions as per the number of chicken fillets.
4. Place one flattened chicken fillet on the chopping board; spread one portion of stuffing evenly; roll it tightly and place on the one cut piece of foil; roll the foil over it covering the sides too. Thus, stuff all the fillets and roll in foil individually.
5. Place rolled packets in the baking tray on the upper shelf of the oven; keep a bowl of water too on the lower shelf and cook by steam and bake method for 45 minutes to 1 hour.
6. Remove and cool the chicken parcels under refrigeration. Unwrap the foil carefully and slice the rolls.

Serving: Arrange the sliced chicken in a flatter dish and cover with the warm mushroom dip. Enjoy the dish cold as part of the cold meal in summers.

If you want to enjoy it hot during winter months, cover it with cling wrap loosely and heat it up in a microwave on REHEAT mode for 3 minutes. Or

Heat the dish in a traditional oven for 15 to 20 minutes after covering it with a piece of aluminum foil.

Variation in usage: You may enjoy the sliced rolls as a starter with Mustard sauce or Tomato sauce. Use them as sandwich fillers. Use them as sandwich fillers.

Tips: The chicken rolls can be prepared a day or two in advance and stored in deep freezer, but should be removed 2 hours before use. Even the mushroom dip can be stored in a chill tray.

Cooking time: 1 hour.

33. Chili-Garlic Flavoured Broccoli

(Broccoletti con peperoncini e agilo)

You Require:

Broccoli	1 head	Garlic chopped	1 tbsp heaped
Chilli flakes	1 tsp	Olive oil	2 tbsp
Salt-n-pepper	to taste		

Preparation and Cooking:

1. Break broccoli in flowerets and steam in a microwave for 3 minutes on HIGH; take out and rinse under the tap immediately, so that it retains the colour.
2. Heat oil and garlic in another bowl for 2 minutes on HIGH; add broccoli, salt, pepper and chilli flakes; stir nicely; cover and cook for 2 minutes. Stand the dish for a couple of minutes and then serve.

   Serving: Serve it hot as a side dish.

   Cooking time: 7 minutes.

34. Garlc Flavoured Prawns Rissotto

(Risotto con agilo e gamberi)

In Italy risotto / rice is served as a separate course, before the meat and vegetables. It makes an excellent starter and many a times is followed by the crisp salad of leaves, as a contrast to its creaminess and to cleanse the plate.

You Require:

Arborio risotto rice	1 and ½ cup	Shelled prawns	2 cups
Oil	3 tbsp	Lemon juice	2 tbsp
Garlic chopped fine	2 tbsp	Mint leaves	¼ cup
Water / stock	3 cups	Salt-n-pepper	to taste
Grated parmesan	¼ cup		

Preparation and Cooking:

1. Wash and soak rice for 30 minutes.
2. Smear prawns with lemon juice, salt and pepper.
3. Chop half the mint and keep aside.
4. Heat oil in a thick bottomed pan and sauté garlic in it; add rice fry for 1 minute; add water / stock, salt and pepper and cook co. Bring the mixture to a boiling point; cover the vessel and cook on medium-low heat for 20 to 25 minutes.

5. Open the pan of rice after 15 minutes; add prawns and chopped mint; stir lightly; cover again and cook for specified period or till the rice is done.
6. At this level add cheese if you like and stir with a fork. Stand for 5 minutes and serve.

   Or

   Serve the shaven or grated cheese along with the rice preparation.

   Serving: Garnish the dish with remaining mint leaves and serve it hot.

   Cooking time: 35 to 40 minutes.

35. Grilled Courgettes with Pines

(Zucchine con pine nuts)

Simple dish of courgettes served as a side dish adds fibre to food.

You Require:

Zucchini/ courgettes	2 no	Pine nuts	about 24 in no
Olive oil	for brushing the zucchini	Salt and Pepper	to taste
Coriander chopped	1 tbsp	Lemon juice	1 tbsp

Preparation and Cooking:

1. Slice zucchini / courgettes in any shape and brush with olive oil, lemon juice salt and pepper, and stand for 15 minutes.
2. Heat your electric grill properly; brush lightly and grill 3 to 4 zucchini pieces in it. Finish grilling all the pieces in the same fashion. Check the seasonings. Arrange in a serving plate.
3. Roast pine nuts in a non-stick pan on medium fire for a minute or two.
4. Garnish the grilled vegetables with roasted pine nuts.

   Serving: Serve it as a side dish along with any non-vegetarian meal.

Tips: Wash and scrub with a kitchen towel, but do not peel zucchini. Cook them as they are sliced in any shape. You may cook the sliced pieces in a heavy non-stick griddle pan.

Cooking time: 20 to 25 minutes.

36. Chicken-balls in Chili-Garlic Sauce

You Require:

For chicken-balls:

Chicken mince	500 gm	Egg	1 no
Parsley chopped	2 tbsp	Clove powder	¼ tsp
Cinnamon powder	¼ tsp	Fresh bread crumbs	½ cup

Olive oil	1 tbsp	Grated cheese	2 tbsp
Salt and pepper	to taste	Green chilli chopped fine	2 no

For Chili Garlic sauce:

Onion chopped fine	1 medium	Garlic chopped	2 tbsp
Red chilli sauce	2 tbsp	Tomato sauce	¼ cup
Paprika	¼ tsp	Olive oil	2 tbsp
Chicken stock	2 cups	Salt	to taste

For serving:

Green, red and yellow peppers1/2 each (opt)

Preparation and Cooking:

1. Cut peppers into cubes and lightly saute with 1 tbsp oil and seasonings. Keep aside
2. Combine all the ingredients for chicken balls and mix properly. Form the small balls from the mixture and place them in the steaming basket of a microwave with ¼ cup water underneath. Steam them for 4 minutes on MEDIUM that is 80% power. Stand them for 3 minutes. You may steam chicken balls in a steamer on gas heat, without a microwave, till done.
3. Meantime, heat oil and fry chopped onions and garlic in it. Add paprika, chilli sauce and tomato sauce, stir and add chicken stock and salt. Cover and cook for 5 to 7 minutes till almost all the liquid has been absorbed by chicken balls.

Serving: Place the chicken balls in the centre of a shallow dish and place peppers around them. Serve hot.

Cooking time: 30 minutes.

37. Lasagne Cooked with Spinach Sauce

(Lasagne conspinaci)

Italians cook Lasagne with a variety of vegetables and meats. This preparation with spinach is quite liked by vegetarians.

You Require:

For spinach sauce:

Spinach puree	2 cups	Tomato puree	½ cup
Cream	¼ cup	Ginger garlic paste	2 tsp
Italian herbs	1 tsp	Brown onion	2 tbsp
Butter	1 tbsp	Chilli garlic	1 tbsp
Salt-n- pepper	to taste		

Other ingredients:

White sauce	1 and ½ cup	Grated cheese	½ cup
Pancakes	6 to 8 no		

Note: Recipe of the pancakes has already been written in **Cannelloni Ripieni.**

Preparation and Cooking:

1. Mix all the ingredients for spinach sauce together. Use it in place of meat sauce (lasagne cooked with meat sauce).
2. Preheat the oven to moderate heat.
3. Smear a rectangular ovenproof dish with a little oil and assemble lasagne.
4. Spread a little spinach sauce in the base of the dish; sprinkle a little grated cheese evenly; cover the base with pancakes; spread cheese sauce thinly over the pancakes; spread spinach sauce and repeat the layers until everything is consumed. Top it with pancakes and grate cheese over them.
5. Bake it in hot oven for 30 to 35 minutes or until dish is nicely heated through and cheese on top is sizzling.

Serving: Serve it hot as a main meal dish.

Tips: This sumptuous dish of layered pasta is a delight for vegetarian and a complete meal in itself, therefore, other accompaniments can be lighter in nature.

Cooking time: 45 to 50 minutes when pancakes are ready.

38. Peppers Cooked in Rome Style

(Peperonata alla romana)

A classic dish of peppers cooked in a typical Italian style is relished as a side dish any time.

You Require:

Peppers of any colour	3 no	Onion sliced	1 no
Garlic sliced	2 fat cloves	Tomatoes	3 to 4 no
Wine vinegar	2 tbsp	Cinnamon powder	¼ tsp (opt)
Freshly ground pepper	to taste	Salt	to taste
Capers	1 to 2 tbsp	Olive oil	3 tbsp

Preparation and Cooking:

1. Roast peppers, sweat in a plastic bag, peel and slice.
2. Roast, peel, deseed and chop tomatoes.
3. Heat oil in a pan, sauté onions and garlic till pinkish; add sliced peppers and cook until tender.

4. Add tomatoes and stir; splash wine vinegar and sprinkle salt and pepper powder; and cook until tomatoes are tender.
5. Remove and add capers. Sprinkle cinnamon and stir.

   Serving: Serve the dish hot with any bread.

   Cooking time: 30 minutes.

39.Tagliated Mushroom Pasta with Mushroom Sauce

A delicacy made of mushroom pasta with mushroom sauce is a perfect dish for main course menu. If served with any dry dish of fish or chicken and a vegetable soup, this pasta dish is an excellent accompaniment to any Italian menu.

You Require:

Mushroom pasta	250 gm	Mushrooms	300 gm
Garlic chopped fine	2 tbsp	Tomato puree	1 cup
Onion chopped fine	1 medium	Basil chopped	2 tbsp
Parsley chopped	1 tbsp		
Olives green / black (pitted and chopped)	2 tbsp	Extra virgin Olive oil	50 ml
Salt-n-pepper	to taste	Grated cheese	¼ cup (opt)

Preparation and Cooking:

1. Clean the mushroom well and slice.
2. Cook mushroom pasta in plenty of boiling salted water in which a few drops of cooking oil are also incorporated till crisply done. Drain hot water and rinse pasta under tap water. Place it in a large serving bowl and sprinkle 2 tbsp olive oil on it; mix lightly with a hand; cover it and keep warm.
3. Heat remaining olive oil in a pan and sauté chopped onion and garlic in it; add tomato puree and chopped basil; cook for 2 minutes and add sliced mushroom. Stir nicely and add 1 cup water, salt and pepper to taste; cover the pan and cook for 10 minutes on low fire.
4. Add the mushroom sauce to the cooked pasta and mix well with a light hand.

   Serving: Serve it hot garnished with chopped parsley, olives and grated cheese.

   Cooking time: 35 minutes.

40. Stuffed Tomatoes with Pasta

You Require:

Firm and ripe tomatoes	6 no. medium

Or

Small tomatoes	12 no	Small soup pasta	100 gm
Black Olives sliced	6 no	Coriander-basil chopped	¼ cup
Parmesan cheese grated	¼ cup	Olive oil	3 tbsp
Salt-n-pepper	to taste	Italian seasonings	to taste

Preparation and Cooking:

1. Wash and dry tomatoes; slice off the tops; with the help of a small spoon scoop out the pulp; sprinkle salt lightly inside the tomatoes and invert them on the rack to drain well.
2. Chop the pulp and place in a strainer.
3. Cook soup pasta in boiling salted water; drain and smear with a little olive oil.
4. Preheat the oven to 190 degrees Celsius, and brush a baking tray well with oil.
5. Combine all the ingredients for stuffing the tomatoes in a bowl; add tomato pulp and cooked pasta, and check the seasonings. Stuff the empty shells of tomatoes with the mixture and place in the baking tray.
6. Bake in the hot oven for 15 to 20 minutes. Stand for 5 minutes.

   Serving: Serve them hot or at a room temperature. You may peel off the skin before eating.

   Cooking time: 30 minutes.

41. Stuffed Cabbage Rolls

Stuffed cabbage rolls make a satisfying side dish to be consumed along with a hearty soup and toasts either at lunch or dinner.

You Require:

Large cabbage leaves	8 no	Fried garlic	1 tbsp
Parsley chopped	¼ cup	Olive oil	1 tbsp
Dry oregano	½ tsp	Chili flakes	½ tsp
Tomato sauce	1 tbsp	Salt	to taste
Cooked mince	1 and ½ cup	Egg	1 no
Or			
Any veg filling			

Preparation and Cooking:

1. Wash and steam cabbage leaves. Place the cabbage in the steaming basket of a microwave with ¼ cup water underneath and cook for 5 minutes on HIGH.

   Or

Blanch them in boiling water for 5 minutes. Remove and rinse under tap water. Drain well and spread them on a kitchen towel to cool. Later dry the leaves with a towel

2. Mix together cooked mince, egg, parsley, fried garlic, oregano, chili flakes, tomato sauce and salt. Divide the mixture into 8 parts.
3. Brush a micro-safe shallow dish with a little olive oil. Brush the working area with oil; place one cabbage leaf on it and spread one portion of filling on it, leaving a border of an inch all around. Fold the sides and start rolling the cabbage leaf upwards. Finish stuffing and rolling all the leaves.
4. Place them in the prepared dish; brush the rolls with oil lightly and cover with cling wrap. Place in a microwave for 3 minutes. Stand the dish for 3 minutes and remove the wrap.

   Or

   You may cook them in a nonstick pan over moderate heat.

   Serving: Serve them warm.

   Cooking time: 40 minutes.

42. Sweet-n-Sour Aubergines (Brinjals)

(Melanzane sweet-n-sour)

One of the most popular dishes in southern part of Italy since olden times; it is cooked a day in advance and served next day so that sweet and sour flavours of the dish develop well.

You Require:

Small aubergines	12 no	Extra virgin olive oil	1 cup
Lemon juice	from 1 lemon	Cloves	4 no
Balsamic vinegar	2 tbsp	Pine nuts	¼ cup
Raisins	3 tbsp	Sugar	1 tbsp
Chili flakes	1 tsp	Pepper powder	1 tsp
Bay leaf	1 no	Salt	to taste

Preparation and Cooking:

1. Preheat the oven to 230 degrees Celsius.
2. Wash, dry and cut aubergines lengthwise.
3. Brush the cut side of the aubergines with a little oil; place them in a baking dish and roast for 30 to 35 minutes, turning them over once in between or until get the brown specs all over.
4. Make the marinade: combine remaining olive oil, lemon juice, vinegar, sugar, clove, salt, pepper and bay leaf; mix well; add pine nuts, raisins and chili flakes mix the marinade once again.

5. Place the hot aubergines in a glass bowl and pour the marinade over them. Keep aside to cool. Cover and store under refrigeration. They stay fresh for a few days.

   Serving: Serve the baby aubergines cold as a side dish.

   Cooking time: 45 to 50 minutes.

43. Chicken Roasted with Wine and Herbs

Chicken and meats are mostly served in Italy as a second course followed by vegetables. Roasting too is done in various ways with different ingredients. The country side, they even use pheasants for roasting.

You Require:

Chicken cut into 8 pieces	1 no.	Red wine	½ cup
Cooking vinegar	1/4 cup	Garlic paste	1 tbsp
Rosemary dry	½ tsp	Oregano	½ tsp
Olive oil / butter	2 tbsp	Passata	1 tbsp
Salt	½ tsp	Pepper powder	1 tsp
Red chilli paste	1 tbsp	Pickled vegetables	2 tbsp
Steamed mixed vegetables for serving		Chicken stock	¼ to ½ cup

Preparation and Cooking:

1. Wash chicken and give slits with a sharp knife. Clean it with kitchen towel and marinate.
2. Mix together vinegar, chili paste, pickled vegetables, passata, garlic and garlic in a blender and blend to paste. Remove the mixture in a bowl and add olive oil or melted butter, herbs and seasonings. Marinate chicken with this. Mixture, rub it nicely on the pieces; cover and stand for 4 to 6 hours, according to weather.
3. Preheat oven to 220 degrees Celsius. Place chicken in a baking tray. Add red wine and chicken stock. Mix the chicken once again.
4. Cover the tray with foil and place it in the oven. Cook it for 30 minutes so that chicken is partially cooked. Bring the tray out from oven; do not switch the oven off; remove foil and stir chicken with a wooden spatula; turn the side of the chicken pieces, baste them well with the mixture and place the tray again in the oven. Cook it uncovered for 35 to 40 minutes. Turn the chicken pieces in between once again (brush them with the mixture and if required sprinkle some chicken stock over chicken) and cook till it is dry.
5. Remove the tray and keep it covered with foil till served It will keep the moisture intact and dish will not be too dry. Leave the tray in the oven if serving within 30 minutes. Reheat slightly if serving late.

Serving: Place the roasted chicken in the serving plate and surround it with steamed vegetables, lightly tossed with a few drops of olive oil.

Note: You may roast the cleaned chicken skinned or dressed.

Cooking time: Approximately 1 hour 15 minutes.

❒

Zuccini with Pesto

DESSERTS

Lemon Souffle

Apple Tart

Amaretti Almond Cookies

Cenci

Choco Roll

Coffee Granita

Fruit Salad

Italian Cookies

Italian Trifle

Tiramisu

Vanilla Custard Ice Cream

Walnut-Orange-Ricota Cake

Zabaglione

Apple Cake

Lemon Cheese Cake

Lemon Ice-cream

Orange Granita

Plain Chocolate Cake

Stuffed Peaches

Baked Apples with Red Wine

Baked Apples with Red Wine Stage-2

Baked Apples with Red Wine Stage-3

Fresh Fruit Figs

Homemade Hazelnut Ice-cream

Sesame Cookies

Desserts

In Italy special desserts are served on special occasions and that too, are brought from the pastry shops or ice cream parlour (if they are cake, pastry and ice cream) known as pasticceria and gelateria respectively. Everyday meals, generally, end with seasonal fresh fruits in one or other form. And other sweet things are popularly enjoyed with a cup of espresso coffee at other times of the day.

1. Lemon Soufflé

(Soufflé-Ala-Milanaise)

You Require:

Milk	300 ml	Eggs	3 no
Cream	1 cup	Sugar	5 tbsp
Gelatin	4 tsp	Lemon	3 no
Lemon rind	from 3 no	Ice-trays with ice	2 no

Aluminium soufflé or custard mould that can hold 4 cup liquid

Preparation and Cooking:

1. Clean mould; smear it with a little cooking oil; rinse with water without touching inside; shake it and place in the deep freezer to chill.
2. Grate the whole lemons with a fine grater to take out the lemon rind; collect it and keep aside. Cut lemons and squeeze the juice.
3. Separate the egg yolks and whites.
4. Boil 1 cup water for 2 minutes on HIGH and dissolve gelatin in it. Mix gelatin\ crystals with 2 tbsp water in a small bowl; place the bowl in boiling hot water and keep stirring till transparent; leave in hot water till used.
5. In a micro-safe bowl mix together egg yolks, sugar and milk; beat with a rotary beater/ eggbeater and cook on HIGH for 2 minutes, stirring once.
6. Now cook egg custard on micro MEDIUM for 4 minutes, stirring every 2 minutes; take it out and mix warm gelatin with it. Stir gelatin once again before mixing with custard. Cool the custard in the following manner:
7. Put enough water in a wide mouthed vessel or trove; place the custard bowl in it to take out the heat; change water and add ice to it; cool custard and keep stirring to avoid any lumps.
8. Add lemon juice, lemon rind and ¾ cup of cream to the custard when it is cold enough.
9. Beat egg whites very stiff and fold into the thickening custard.
10. Pour the mixture in the chilled mould and replace it in the deep freezer for 30 to 40

minutes or till set. Later, place in the refrigerator till used.

Note: Cover the mould with cling film or aluminium foil and leave it in the deep freezer only if it is going to be served after a couple of days but take it out at least 6 hours before use from the freezer and keep in the lower compartment of your refrigerator.

Serving: Loosen the soufflé with butter knife and de-mould it in a chilled plate; cover it with remaining cream and serve immediately. You may cut it in wedges and serve.

Variation: Make Strawberry soufflé. Make egg custard the way it is explained in the recipe; omit lemon juice, rind and gelatin; instead, take one strawberry jelly crystals (packet)and cook with ½ quantity of water (mentioned on the packet) in the microwave for 6 to 7 minutes on HIGH or till jelly crystals are dissolved. Keep stirring every 2 minutes. Now chill the jelly mixture on a pan of ice (the way custard was done) and add egg custard mixture in it. When half set, pour into the chilled mould.

Tips:
1. Cold soufflés for desserts are generally served de-moulded, but you can set them in a glass bowls too, and serve.
2. Always mix dissolved gelatin to the warm liquid, and never to the cold one, otherwise instead of setting the liquid it will turn lumpy or stringy.

Milanaise is also written as Milanese.

Cooking time:8 minutes micro cooking and 30 minutes to cool the custard; mix with other ingredients and place it for setting.

2.Apple Cake

(Torta di mele)

It is a delicious moist cake; it should be enjoyed when still warm. It comes from Genoa.

You Require:

Flour	1 and ½ cup	Powdered sugar	¾ cup
Melted butter	½ cup	Eggs	4 no
Apples	3 no medium	Lemon rind from	1 large lemon
Lemon juice from	1 large lemon	Baking powder	1 tsp
Salt	a pinch	Castor sugar	2 tbsp
Whipped cream	1 cup (opt)		

Orange rind cut into fine strips for garnishing

Preparation and Cooking:

1. Preheat the oven for moderate heat.
2. Prepare a 9-inch baking tin by greasing it and lining the base with non-stick baking sheet.
3. Sieve flour salt and baking powder together.
4. Core and peel the apples. Slice them thinly, place them in a glass bowl and sprinkle them

with lemon juice to avoid dis-colouration.

5. Combine eggs, sugar and grated lemon rind in a mixing bowl and beat with hand held electric beater until the mixture is thick and light.
6. Stir in half the sieved flour and fold in gently with a large spoon. Slowly drizzle in the melted butter and fold it with a light hand; stir in the remaining flour and fold that, too, gently. Now add sliced apples and fold in these too gently.
7. Spoon the mixture into the prepared tin and level the surface and bake for 40 minutes in a preheated oven. Check the doneness by inserting a needle, it should come out clean, otherwise, bake the cake for 5 minutes more.
8. Remove the cake from the oven and let it stand for 15 minutes to settle. Invert it on wire rack.

Serving: Turn the cake; place the right side up in a serving plate and sprinkle the castor sugar over the top. Decorate it with the orange rind strips.

Serve it warm with whipped cream.

Tips: For extra delicious touch add grated lemon rind to the cream while whipping it.

Baking time 40 to 45 minutes.

3. Vanilla Custard Ice-Cream

(Vanilla gelato de crema)

Home-made vanilla ice-cream is very popular in parts of the country; though commercial ice creams are available in plenty but home-made has distinct taste and flavour. This is the basic ice cream for so many different flavours.

You Require:

Full cream milk	2 and½ cups	Sugar	½ cup
Butter	¼ cup	Corn flour	¼ cup
Egg yolks	3 no	Cream	½ cup
Vanilla essence	1 tbsp		

Preparation and Cooking:

1. Place eggs, sugar, corn flour and vanilla essence n a thick-bottomed pan and beat with electric beater until creamy.
2. Heat milk and butter till the butter melts. Pour it over the beaten egg mixture slowly, stirring constantly and thoroughly. Cook the mixture over boiling water or use double boiler, constantly beating till it starts thickening and coating the back of the spoon. Remove from the fire and cool.
3. Whip the cream and fold into the custard.
4. Freeze the mixture until firm, say after about 4 to 5 hours. Remove it from the freezing tray; chop it roughly and beat with the electric mixer until smooth.

5. Return the ice-cream to the freezer tray once again and freeze until firm. You may repeat the process of chopping and beating it once more to get very smooth consistency.

Serving: Serve it as and when required.

Variation: Make Chocolate ice cream. Melt 150 gm of cooking chocolate and add to the vanilla ice-cream at Step-2 while cooking the custard. Rest follow the same procedure.

Tips: Ice cream can be prepared a couple of days in advance. Quantity can be doubled or increased as per your requirement.

Cooking time: 30 minutes and freezing time extra.

4.Stuffed Peaches

(Pesche ripiene)

Fresh fruits are enjoyed as desserts too. They are eaten as such or in various other ways. This recipe is one of the specimens.

You Require:

Firm peaches	4 to 6 no	Almond cookies	6 to 8 no
Butter softened	2 tbsp	Castor sugar	2 tbsp
Egg yolk	1 to 2 no	Raisins / sultanas	2 tbsp
Amaretto liqueur (brandy)	4 tbsp	White wine	1 cup
Basil sprig and leaves			
Fresh cream or vanilla ice-cream to serve with			

Preparation and Cooking:

1. Preheat the oven to 180 degrees Celsius.
2. Grease lightly a baking dish.
3. Cut each peach into half down to the central stone, twist the peach in opposite direction to separate it. Thus remove the stones from all peaches. With a teaspoon scoop each half a little to make a little more place for stuffing. Chop the scooped flesh and keep aside to be used later.
4. Crush the almond cookies with a pestle and mortar or a rolling pin nicely. Chop the sultanas.
5. Cream together butter and sugar until smooth; stir in egg yolk, chopped flesh of the fruit, sultanas, half of the brandy and crushed cookies.
6. Spoon the prepared stuffing into the peaches and set them in the baking dish.
7. Combine remaining brandy and white wine together and pour over the peaches.
8. Bake for 25 to 30 minutes or until peaches appear tender if tested with a skewer.

Serving: Garnish with basil and serve immediately with cream or ice-cream.

Cooking time: 45 minutes.

5. Lemon- Cheese Cake

(Torta di limone e ricotta)

A variety of cheese cakes is an integral part of Italian cuisine and most of them are prepared with ricotta cheese in different combinations.

You Require:

Flour	1 and ½ cup	Granulated sugar	¾ cup
Eggs	3 no	Ricotta cheese	1/3 cup
Butter	1/3 cup	Baking powder	1 and ½ tsp
Lemon-juice	3 tbsp	Lemon rind	1 tsp
Icing sugar for dusting			

Preparation and Cooking:

1. Pre heat the oven to 180 degrees Celsius.
2. Prepare the baking mould; line the bottom with waxed paper; grease and dust it with flour.
3. Sieve together flour and baking powder.
4. Separate the egg whites.
5. Cream the butter and sugar together until smooth. Beat in the ricotta cheese. Beat in the egg yolks one by one Add 2 tbsp flour, lemon juice and rind; mix thoroughly; and beat in the remaining flour until well blended.
6. Beat the egg whites stiff and fold them gently into the batter.
7. Pour the mixture into the prepared baking mould and bake it for 45 minutes. Check the doneness by inserting a needle and that should come out clean.
8. Remove from the oven and let it cool for 15 minutes. Invert it on cooling rack.
9. Dust the cake nicely with icing sugar before serving.

Serving: Cut the Lemon-Cheese-Cake into wedges and serve.

Cooking time: 55 to 60 minutes.

6. Baked Apples With Red Wine

(Mele al forno)

You Require:

Cooking apples	6 no	Red wine	1 and ½ cup
Sultanas / raisins	½ cup	Sugar	5 tbsp
Nutmeg powder	a pinch	Cinnamon powder	a pinch
Lemon rind	½ tsp	Butter	3 tbsp

Preparation and Cooking:

1. Combine red wine, sugar, sultanas, nutmeg, cinnamon and lemon rind in a bowl and keep it aside for 1 hour.
2. Preheat oven for 200 degrees Celsius. Butter a baking dish large enough to hold the apples.
3. Wash, wipe and core apples without damaging their bottoms. Remove the central cores and arrange them in the buttered dish.
4. Divide the soaked sultanas' mixture in 6 parts and spoon in the cavity (hollows created in the apples) of the apples; spoon in extra spiced wine also and pour the remaining wine around the apples.
5. Top each apple with a knob of butter and bake for 40 to 45 minutes or until the apples are soft. Apples may appear a little shrunk but should not disintegrate. Remove from the oven.

Serving: Serve the apples in individual plates either hot or at room temperature. Spoon some more, thickened, wine over the apples before serving because spiced-thickened wine is the tastiest part of this dessert and the fun lies in licking it while enjoying the fruit.

Cooking time: 1 hour 15 minutes.

7. Walnut-Orange-Ricotta Cake

You Require:

Self-raising flour	½ cup	Sugar powdered	2/3rd cup
Eggs separated	5 no	Butter	½ cup
Walnuts shelled	2/3rd cup	Orange rind	from 1 orange
Ricotta cheese	2/3rd cup		
Finishing and Garnishing:			
Orange marmalade	3 tbsp	Brandy / Rum	1 tbsp
Grated chocolate		Chocolate curls / chips	
Fresh orange segments			

Preparation and Cooking:

1. Preheat the oven to 190 degrees Celsius.
2. Prepare the mould by greasing and lining it.
3. Chop the walnuts roughly; put in a paper bag and toast for 1 minute on HIGH.
4. Place softened butter and sugar in a working bowl and cream till light and fluffy. Add egg yolks, orange rind and ricotta cheese, and mix. Now add sieved flour and walnut pieces, and mix again.
5. Beat egg whites very stiff and fold in the cake mixture.
6. Put the mixture into the prepared baking mould; level the surface and bake for 35 minutes

or until firm. Cool the cake in the tin for 30 minutes or so, and then transfer it to a serving plate.

7. Meantime heat the marmalade with 1 tbsp water; mix and add brandy or rum. Coat the top and the sides of the cake with it and cover it with grated chocolate.

Serving: Garnish the cake with chocolate curls / chips and fresh orange segments. Cut into pieces and serve.

Cooking time: 50 minutes.

8. Orange Granita

(Granita all'arancia)

Orange ganita is a refreshing dessert after a rich main course. It is like a water ice, but coarser and grainy as its name suggests. This cooling treat is excellent in hot summer months.

You Require:

Oranges	6 no	Lemon rind	from 1-lemon
Sugar	¾ cup	Water	2 cups
Orange and lemon rind to decorate			

Preparation and Cooking:

1. Chill a freezer tray.
2. Squeeze the juice from the oranges and keep aside.
3. Cut open the 2 orange peels into 2 parts and with a fruit knife scrape all the white bitter pith from inside; cut the peel in very thin stripes and keep aside.
4. Heat sugar and water together, stirring over medium heat, till the sugar dissolves; then boil the mixture till it turns into syrup.
5. Remove it from the fire and add the orange and lemon rinds. Shake the pan well, cover and allow it to cool.
6. Strain the sugar syrup and mix it with orange juice. Stir well and pour into the chilled freezer tray and freeze uncovered for almost 3 to 4 hours or until slushy.
7. Remove the half set ice from the freezer; mix it with a fork and then freeze it again for 4 to 5 hours or until frozen hard.

Serving: Turn the orange ice into a bowl and soften it for 10 to 15 minutes; break it with a fork again and pile up into the stemmed glasses. Decorate with the strips of orange and lemon rind.

Serve with dessert biscuits.

Variation: Make lemon ice.

Preparation time: 8 to 9 hours.

9. Tiramisu

(Tiramisu)

Tiramisu is a cool and refreshing popular Italian dessert made from sponge-fingers, espresso coffee, mascarpone cheese, eggs, cream, sugar, Marsala wine and cocoa. It is made of sweet cream layered on top of ladyfinger cookies soaked with coffee or liqueur and finished by sprinkling cocoa on top. It really makes you swoon once you taste it. Its literal meaning explains it better as it says 'pick me up'.

You Require:

Italian sponge fingers	20 to 22 no	Eggs separated	3 no
Mascarpone cheese	2 cups	Flavoured liqueur	½ cup
Or			
Soft home made cheese			
Strong black coffee	1 cup	Vanilla sugar	as much required
Coco powder and dark chocolate to finish the dish			

Preparation:

1. Mix the coffee and liqueur together in a shallow dish and keep aside.
2. Put the egg whites in a bowl and whisk with an electric egg beater until form the peaks.
3. Mix the cheese, vanilla sugar and egg yolks in a separate large bowl and whisk with the electric mixer until evenly mixed. Fold in the egg whites.
4. Put a few spoons full of the mixture in the bottom of a large serving bowl and evenly spread it out.
5. Dip a sponge finger in the mixture and quickly place on top of the cheese mixture in the bowl. Take more sponge fingers dipped in coffee and place by its side, so that cheese mixture is covered.
6. Spoon in about one third of the remaining mixture over the fingers and spread it out.
7. Make more layers the same way ending with cheese mixture. Level the surface.
8. Sift cocoa powder all over the dish. Cover it with a foil loosely and chill it overnight.

Serving: Sprinkle the dish with cocoa powder and grated chocolate before serving.

Preparation time: About 40 minutes.

10. Fruit salad

(Macedonia)

Fresh seasonal fruits are always very refreshing and soothing before / after any meal, and Italy is no exception. Italians, too, enjoy seasonal fruits in the form of ices, salads and desserts thoroughly. You can use any mixture of seasonal fruits, particularly, for this salad.

You Require:

Apple	1 no	Pear	1 no
Strawberries	10 to 12 no	Raspberries	10 to 12 no
Seedless grapes black	½ cup	Seedless green grapes	½ cup
Fresh juice from	3 oranges	Lemon juice	from 1 lemon
Powdered sugar	1 tbsp (opt)		

Preparation:

1. Combine orange-juice, lemon juice and sugar together; mix thoroughly and pour in a large bowl.
2. Prepare all the fruits by washing, peeling and cleaning. Cut the apple and pear into bite size pieces and immediately put in the orange juice to avoid de-colouration; halve / quarter strawberries and raspberries and cut grapes into halves (if required) and mix with the other cut fruits.
3. Lightly mix them with a fork and arrange in a serving bowl. Cover it with a piece of foil or cling wrap and refrigerate at least for 2 hours before serving.

   Serving: Serve it chilled with Vanilla ice-cream.

   Tips: Mostly Italians eat fresh fruit salad alone. Usually, it is not served with cream.

   Preparation time: 30 minutes, chilling time extra.

11.Cenci

(Rags and tatters)

A variety of cookies is an integral part of Italian cuisine which are consumed at festivities, carnivals or anytime in day to day life. Cenci is also one of the varieties. The literal meaning of Cenci is 'rags and tatters' and these interesting pieces are eaten at carnival time.

You Require:

Plain flour / maida	1 and ½ cup	Castor sugar	2 tbsp
Baking powder	½ tsp	Rum	2 tbsp
Egg beaten	1 large	Butter	1 tbsp (opt)
Vegetable oil for deep frying		Icing sugar for dusting	

Preparation and Cooking:

1. Sieve together flour, baking powder, salt and castor sugar in a bowl.
2. Add the butter and mix; add beaten egg and mix with a fork or with your hands until evenly mixed; sprinkle rum evenly and gather flour until it takes the shape of dough.
3. Knead the dough on a lightly floured platform until it is smooth. Divide the dough in three parts.

4. Roll each piece into a thick rectangle sheet / chapatti and cut it lengthwise into strips and tie each strip into a knot. Repeat the process with remaining 2 parts also.
5. Heat oil in a deep frying pan / deep fat fryer or a kadai and check the temperature of the oil. (Drop a piece of dough trimmings and it should be crisp and golden within 30 seconds).
6. Deep fry the knots in small batches for 1 to 2 minutes on medium fire until crisp and golden.
7. Remove with a slotted spoon on kitchen oil absorbent paper.

Serving: Serve the tatters warm after dusting them with icing-sugar.

Cooking time: 45 minutes.

12. Italian Cookies

You Require:

All purpose flour	2 and ½ cups	Sugar	1 tbsp
Lemon rind	1 tsp	Vanilla	1 tsp
Salt	½ tsp	Eggs beaten	4 no
Oil for deep-frying		Honey	1 cup
Candy sprinklers	for garnishing		

Preparation and Cooking:

1. Combine sugar, lemon rind, vanilla and salt in a large bowl.
2. Add eggs and half the flour; stir well; mix in the remaining flour and make soft dough. Knead well.
3. Divide the flour into 20 to 24 pieces; with your hands roll each piece into a pencil shape. Cut each pencil into ½ -inch pieces.
4. Heat oil and fry all the pieces in oil till golden brown and place in a large bowl.
5. Heat honey to a boiling point; pour over cookies and mix well.
6. With a slotted spoon, spoon the cookies on to a serving platter and slowly mound in a tree shape, if you desire so.

Serving: Decorate the cookies with candy sprinklers. Cool them completely before serving.

Cooking time: 45 to 60 minutes.

13. Sesame Cookies

You Require:

All purpose flour	2 cups	Eggs	2 large
Baking powder	2 tsp	Sugar	¾ cup

Butter	1/3 cup	Vanilla essence	1 tsp
Salt	¼ tsp	Milk	½ cup
Sesame seeds	¾ cup		

Preparation and Cooking:

1. Preheat the oven to 180 degrees Celsius. Lightly brush a baking tray with a little oil and keep aside.
2. Sieve flour, baking powder and salt together.
3. In a bowl beat butter and sugar till creamy; add eggs one by one and stir well; now start mixing flour in it, and when all the flour gathers, knead the dough on working surface with your hands.
4. Roll the dough into a long sausage shape and cut into even sized portions. Roughly roll each portion on hand; dip it in the milk and coat with sesame seeds. Finish rolling and coating all the portions; arrange them in the baking tray and bake for 25 to 30 minutes. Switch off the oven and let the cookies stand in for 15 minute more.
5. Cool the cookies and store them in a glass jar.

Note: You may grind half the sesame seeds and add to the flour before making dough and baking. If you are using salted butter for baking, do not add ¼ tsp salt mentioned in the ingredients.

Serving: Serve them at tea time.

Cooking time: 40 to 45 minutes.

14. Coffee Granita

You Require:

Coffee	1 cup strong	Water	2 cups
Sugar	½ to ¾ cup	Cream for garnishing	optional

Preparation and Cooking:

1. Heat the water and sugar together on medium fire until the sugar dissolves fully well. Boil the mixture once and remove from fire. Leave it to cool.
2. Combine coffee and sugar together and pour in the freezer's tray or in a not so deep container. Freeze it until solid.
3. After 2 to 3 hours remove the frozen mixture; turn it out on the chopping board by plunging the bottom of the tray in very hot water for a few seconds.
4. Chop the coffee ice and place it in a food processor with metal blades and process until it turns into the crystals. Or beat it with an electric hand beater till slushy but not watery. Now it is ready to serve.

Note: If you are not serving granita immediately put it back in a container with a lid and freeze till serving.

Serving: Spoon the processed coffee ice into the serving glasses and top with whipped cream.

Cooking time: 30 minutes, freezing time can vary from 3 to 4 hours.

15. Choco Roll

(chocolate salami)

A dark chocolate and almonds based rich after dinner sweetmeat which is not only very tasty but also satisfying.

You Require:

Marie biscuits	24 no	Plain dark chocolate	350 gm
Butter unsalted	225 gm	Egg yolks	2 no
Ground almonds	¼ cup	Roasted almonds slivers	½ cup
Amaretto liqueur	60 ml		
Or			
Rum	¼ cup		
+			
Almond essence	2 drops		

Preparation and Cooking:

1. Coarsely crush biscuits in a processor or dry grinder.
2. Break chocolate into pieces.
3. Place chocolate in a large heatproof bowl and melt it placing over the saucepan of barely simmering water; add a small chunk of the butter and liqueur; and heat until chocolate melts thoroughly, stirring once or twice.
4. Remove the bowl from the heat; allow the chocolate to cool foe a minute or two; stir in the egg yolks and then the remaining butter a little by little. Add most of the crushed biscuits and stir well. Save the remaining biscuits for later use. Stir in the shredded almonds. Keep it aside minimum for 1 hour or till the mixture begins to stiffen.
5. Process the remaining crushed biscuits in the food processor until they are finely ground. Mix with the ground almonds. Cover and keep aside.
6. Place the chocolate mixture on a lightly oiled sheet of greaseproof paper and then shape into a long sausage with a palette knife; wrap in the paper and freeze for at least 6 hours.
7. For serving unwrap the roll; spread the ground biscuits and almond powder on a clean sheet of grease-proof paper and roll the chocolate sausage until evenly coated. Leave it to stand for 1 hour.

Serving: Cut it in thin slices before serving and serve it with espresso coffee or liqueur.

Cooking time: The whole process will take about 6 to 7 hours,

16. Apple Tart

Awesome apple tart, not only satisfies the sweet tooth but also gives lots of energy, and it is just ideal for the cold weather.

You require:

For tart shell:

Flour	1 and 1/2 cup	Butter	1/2 cup - 3 tbsp
Chilled water		Salt	1/4 tsp

For filling:

Green apples	3 no / 500 gm	Sugar	1/4 cup
Brown sugar	¼ cup	Lemon juice	1 tbsp
Cinnamon powder	1 tbsp	Corn flour	2 tbsp

Preparation and Cooking:

1. Peel and thinly slice apples in a bowl; sprinkle lemon juice, both the sugars and cinnamon powder. Mix well; cover and keep aside for 2 hours.
2. Meantime, make short crust pastry dough. Sieve flour and salt together; mix butter with your finger tips till the mixture resembles breadcrumbs; add water and make dough. If required, sprinkle a few more drops of cold water to hold the ingredients together. Knead it well to pliable dough.

   Note: In summers wrap the dough in cling film and refrigerate for 20 minutes before rolling.
3. Divide the dough into 2 parts. Keep 1 part wrapped and start rolling the 2nd part on working platform. Sprinkle a little flour on working surface and start rolling the 1 part of dough evenly and line the pie dish with it. Trim the extra dough from the rims of pie dish and prick the base of pie lightly with a fork. Cover it loose and refrigerate. Roll the 2nd part of dough also and refrigerate.
4. Strain the liquid from the apples and save it. Keep the apples in a strainer for 30 minutes and then sprinkle corn flour on them. Meantime reduce the saved liquid; put it in a small micro-safe bowl and cook in a microwave on HIGH, uncovered.
5. Remove that sweet apple liquid from oven and mix it with sliced apples.
6. Take out the lined pie dish and second part of rolled pastry from the refrigerator. Put apples on the pastry dish and cover the top with second part of rolled pastry either as single covering or in a lattice style. Pinch the rims so that upper and lower pastries join together nicely. Trim extra dough if any.

Note: Make 4 to 5 gashes with knife on top of the pastry (if it is a single covering) and bake the pie in a preheated oven at 200 degree Celsius for 40 to 45 minutes. Stand it in the oven for 5 minutes

Serving: Cut it into the wedges and serve it warm.

Cooking time: 45 minutes.

17. Lemon Ice Cream with Walnuts

You Require:

Fresh cream	1and ½ cup	Eggs	3 no
Sugar	1 cup	Lemon juice	2 tbsp
Glucose Biscuit crumbs	1 and ½ cup	Crushed walnuts	¾ cup
Salted butter	¼ cup		

Preparation:

1. Beat 1 whole egg and 2 yolks. Save the whites.
2. Add lemon-juice and sugar to the eggs and beat till creamy and cook on double boiler till the mixture thickens. Or boil water in a large pan and place the vessel with egg and sugar mixture in it and keep stirring with a wooden spoon till it starts coating the back of the spoon. Cool.
3. Beat saved egg whites till they stand on peaks and mix with cooked egg mixture and whipped cream.
4. Mix together the biscuit crumbs, butter and crushed walnuts well.
5. Press half the crumb-walnut mixture in the ice cream tray; pour the lemon cream mixture on top and spread evenly; now spread rest of the crumb mixture on top and press lightly, so that surface appears smooth.
6. Place the ice cream tray in the deep freezer for 3 hours minimum.

Serving: Cut into bars or cubes and serve.

Preparation time: 4 hours.

18. Italian Trifle

You Require:

For Base:

Italian sponge fingers (Savoyard)	200 gm	Rum	1/3rd cup
Or		Or	
Sponge cake	200 gm	Cherry brandy	½ cup

For custard sauce:

Warm milk	2 cups	Egg yolks	2 no
Sugar	4 tbsp	Custard powder	1 tbsp

Butter	1 tbsp	Lemon rind	from ½ scrubbed lemon
For Topping:			
Fresh cream	100 ml	Fresh fruit of your choice	
Toasted nuts chopped			

Preparation and Cooking:

1. Beat together egg yolk, sugar and custard powder in a heavy bottomed sauce pan with egg beater till creamy; add milk slowly and keep beating.
2. Cook on medium fire, stirring all the time with a wooden spoon till the custard starts coating back of the spoon. Remove from fire and add butter; mix properly and add lemon rind. Add 1 tbsp brandy if using. Cover the custard to avoid skin formation and let it cool at platform.
3. In a serving dish arrange the sponge fingers or sponge cake sliced into 1-inch pieces. Sprinkle cherry brandy or rum. Pour the custard slowly covering the whole base. Pour the fresh cream on top.
4. Cover the dish with foil or cling wrap and refrigerate it minimum for 2 hours.
5. Decorate it with sliced fresh fruit and chopped toasted nuts.

Serving: Serve it cold with or without a swirl of additional cream.

Tips: You may brush the sponge fingers with a little hot jam slightly thinned before adding custard. You may avoid brandy or rum and use thin chocolate sauce.

Variation:

1. Cut 1-chocolate sponge into 2 halves.
2. Soak the halves with thin chocolate sauce.
3. Spread commercial vanilla ice cream in ½ inch thick layer on one of the half.
4. Place the second half on top.
5. Sprinkle some chocolate sauce on top and nicely cover it with ice-cream. Refrigerate for ½ an hour.
6. Decorate it with chocolate chips and chocolate sauce.

Note: In this book, the variation has been photographed.

Preparation time: 45 minutes.

19. Home-Made Hazelnut Ice Cream

A popular dessert enjoyed anytime, anywhere by young and old alike.

You Require:

One recipe	Vanilla custard ice cream
Hazelnuts	½ cup
Sugar	2 tbsp

Preparation and Cooking:

1. Crush the hazelnuts with sugar.
2. Add to the vanilla custard ice cream mixture when it is being cooked over simmering water and before the custard thickens. Cool.
3. Whip the cream and fold into the custard.
4. Freeze the mixture until firm (about 4 to 5 hours).
5. Remove it from the freezing tray; chop it roughly and beat with the electric mixer until smooth.
5. Return the ice-cream to the freezer tray once again and freeze until firm. You may repeat the process of chopping and beating it once more to get very smooth consistency.

   Serving: Serve it as and when required.

   Cooking time: 30 minutes and freezing time extra.

20. Zabaglione

(zabaglione)

This warm dessert is quick to make but it needs to be served straight away. It should be made the last moment.

You Require:

Egg yolks	5 no	Castor sugar	¼ cup
Marsala	½ cup	Long stemmed glasses	6 no
Italian sponge fingers to serve			

Preparation and Cooking:

1. Take a large pan, half fill with water and boil it, lower the heat.
2. Put egg yolks and sugar in a heatproof large bowl and beat with the hand electric beater until creamy.
3. Now place the bowl over the pan of simmering hot water and pour in marsala wine, whisking the mixture until very thick and has increased in volume.
4. Remove the bowl from the heat and pour the zabaglione mixture into glasses.

   Serving: Serve the dessert at once with sponge fingers

   Cooking time: 10 to 15 minutes.

21. Chocolate Cake

Plain-rich Chocolate cake can be enjoyed with tea / coffee. It can also be enjoyed with ice-cream.

You Require:

Flour	2 and ½ cups	Sugar	1 and ½ cup
Cocoa powder	¾ cup	Butter	¾ cup
Baking powder	½ tsp	Baking soda	1 and ½ tsp
Eggs	2 number	Warm milk	1 cup
Rum	¼ cup (opt)		

Preparation and Cooking:

1. Preheat an oven to 180 degrees Celsius. Prepare a 9-inch cake mould; line it with thick brown paper and brush with melted butter.
2. Sieve together flour, cocoa, baking soda and baking powder twice or thrice.
3. Powder sugar if the granules are bigger.
4. Cream together butter and sugar; add eggs and beat. Add warm milk and beat thoroughly with electric beater. Add sieved flour spoon by spoon and keep mixing. Add rum. Mix thoroughly and pour in the cake mould.
5. Make a depression in the centre and bake it in the hot oven for 45 to 50 minutes.
6. Check the done-ness with cake needle, it should come out clean, otherwise cook for 5 minutes more. Leave in the oven for 5 minutes.
7. Remove and cool for 15 minutes and then invert on cooling rack.

Serving: Serve it warm or at room temperature.

Tips: Cool it thoroughly before storing it. Stored under refrigeration, it becomes richer in colour and taste; and lasts for more than a month.

Variation: You can add roughly crushed walnuts / Hazelnuts or almonds to the cake for enriched taste.1/2 to ¾ cup of nuts will do wonders.

Cooking time: 1 hour.

22. Almond Cookies

(Amaretti)

Amaretti-the classic Italian almond cookies are made of sweet almonds + bitter almonds but since bitter almonds are not easily available, these can be cooked with sweet almonds only. These cookies when hot are crispy on the outside and a little chewy on the outside, once completely cool, get crunchy, but are delicious in taste, and excellent with any fruit dessert.

You Require:

Blanched Almonds	2 cup	Castor sugar	1 cup
Egg white	2 no.	Almond extract	½ tsp
Vanilla essence	¼ tsp	Icing sugar for dusting	

Preparation and Cooking:

1. Place blanched almonds in a baking tray and let them dry in a moderately hot oven for 10 minutes. Take out the tray. Cool the almonds.
2. Grind the almonds with half the sugar, add remaining sugar and continue beating for a few seconds. Add almonds and both the essence, and mix once again. Take the mixture out of the food processor.
3. Preheat the oven to 160 degrees Celsius
4. Form the small balls out of the mixture and place in the baking tray lined with greased paper. Or spoon the mixture in the baking tray. Lightly sprinkle icing sugar over the cookies.
5. Bake the almond cookies for 25 to 30 minutes or until golden in colour.
6. Remove the tray from the oven and cool. You may store them in an air-tight jar once completely cool.

Serving: Cookies can be enjoyed anytime, with a beverage or with any fruit dessert after a meal.

Baking time: 25 to 30 minutes.

❑❑❑

Assorted Cookies

Other Books *by the* Author

9788178061344 • ₹ 125

9788178061443 • ₹ 125

9788178060989 • ₹ 96

9788178062198 • ₹ 160

9788178063027 • ₹ 150

Also available online at:

www.unicornbooks.in • www.flipkart.com • www.infibeam.com • www.amazon.in • www.paytm.com

पाक-कला की श्रेष्ठ पुस्तकें

9788178061245 • 150

हमारे उत्सवों एवं त्योहारों में मिष्टान्न का बहुत महत्व है। भगवान को भोग लगाना है तो मिठाई चाहिए, कोई खुशी का अवसर है तो मिठाई चाहिए। करवा चौथ पर मीठी पूरी बननी है, अहोई अष्टमी पर मीठे पुए बनने हैं, होली पर गुझिया बननी है, छठ पर्व पर ठेकुआ बनना है, देवी को भोग लगाना है तो हलुआ बनना ही है। व्रत-उपवास में फलाहारी व्यंजन चाहिए। अतः शुद्धता, पवित्रता की दृष्टि से भी घरेलू मिष्टान्न का अपना महत्व है।

लेखिका ने इस पुस्तक में करीब-करीब हर अवसर पर बनने वाली 166 मिठाइयां, नाश्ते, नमकीन, हलुए आदि को बनाने की विधियां बताई हैं और साथ ही साथ यथास्थान जरूरी टिप्स और हिन्ट्स भी दिए हैं।

कामकाजी महिलाएं जिनके पास समय की कमी है और जिन्हें आरंभिक जानकारी नहीं है, वे भी इन्हें सहजता से बना सकेंगी।

इस प्रकार की भारत में छपने वाली यह पहली पुस्तक है, जिसमें घरेलू मिठाइयों को बनाने का इतना विस्तृत वर्णन है।

स्वादिष्ट भोजन छह प्रकार के स्वादों वाला : मीठा, नमकीन, कड़वा, तीखा, कसैला और खट्टा होता है। अचार, चटनी, मुरब्बे, जैम, जैली वगैरह में कोई एक या एक से अधिक स्वाद अर्थात् रस अवश्य होता है। हर कोई स्वादिष्ट भोजन खाना चाहता है, लेकिन आजकल किसी के पास ठहरकर सोचने का समय नहीं है, न ध्यान देने का समय है, पर स्वादिष्ट भोजन की इच्छा सभी को रहती है।

अचार, चटनी, मुरब्बे, जैम, जैली खाने में स्वाद की सृष्टि करते हैं, नवीनता लाते हैं। इन्हें बनाने की सहज, सरल, सुबोध विधिया इस पुस्तक में जरूरी टिप्स के साथ दी गयी हैं, जो बिना किसी झंझट के बनायी जा सकती हैं और इन्हें कोई भी आसानी से बना सकता है। कौन सब्जी या फल किस मौसम में अच्छा मिलेगा और ठीक मसाला कैसे चुनें, इसकी भी जानकारी इस पुस्तक में दी गयी है। यह पुस्तक हर किसी के लिए उपयोगी है।

छह ऋतुएं होती हैं, हर ऋतु में किसी न किसी फल व सब्जी की बहुतायत होती है। अतः मौसम के समय अच्छे फल व सब्जी चुनकर उन्हें जैम, जैली, अचार, मुरब्बे के रूप में संरक्षित कर, हर मौसम में बदलते स्वादों का आप आनन्द ले सकते हैं। पूर्ण जानकारी से युक्त, स्वाद से भरपूर रोचक शैली में यह पुस्तक लिखी गयी है।

9788178063041 • 150

Also available online at:

www.unicornbooks.in • www.flipkart.com • www.infibeam.com • www.amazon.in • www.paytm.com